"J.D. is clear ... us. He's written a book that's goo ... e, the Christian tempted to legal ... t, the Christian tempted to selfis ... d faithful, reaching out while holding fast, this book will encourage you."
—Mark Dever, senior pastor, Capitol Hill Baptist Church and author of *Nine Marks of a Healthy Church*

"With this book J.D. Greear solidifies his position on a team of young evangelical voices calling the twenty-first century church back to the gospel. He powerfully and probingly shows that the gospel is just as necessary and relevant after you become a Christian as it is before because the gospel doesn't simply rescue us from the past and rescue us for the future; it also rescues us in the present from being enslaved to things like fear, insecurity, anger, self-reliance, bitterness, entitlement, and insignificance. J.D. makes the clear case that when the word of the gospel—Christ's love for us without strings attached—grips our hearts, it sets us free and changes everything."
—Tullian Tchividjian, pastor of Coral Ridge Presbyterian Church, Ft. Lauderdale, Florida, and author of *Jesus + Nothing = Everything*

"My soul continues to be encouraged by the stirring up of strong voices to point people to the gospel and what appears to be a genuine movement back to that thing that Paul considers "of first importance." J.D. has done a masterful job of clarifying and wringing out the gospel implications for the life of the believer. Whether you are a pastor, have been in church your whole life, or have recently become a Christian you will find this book to be helpful."
—Matt Chandler, lead pastor, The Village Church

"My fellow pastor, J.D. Greear, through his book, has helped us in this quest for gospel-saturated living. He takes the principles of gospel centrality and shows us how to orient our lives around it. I appreciate how in refreshing and real ways he makes the gospel accessible to others so that they can experience its transforming power. I especially like the book's practical section on gospel prayer as a way to assist us in rehearsing these truths deep into our hearts and minds. Whether you are exploring Christianity for the first time or are longing to 'look into these things' again and again, let me invite you to spend time with this helpful book."
—Timothy Keller, senior pastor, Redeemer Presbyterian Church and author of *The Reason for God*

"Radical obedience to the person of Christ can only spring from reckless trust in the sufficiency of Christ. I am grateful to God for my friend J.D. Greear and his call to plant our lives and churches solidly in the soil of the gospel. This book will help you rest daily in God's great grace as you live continually for God's great glory."

—David Platt, senior pastor, The Church at Brook Hills
and author of *Radical*

"With disarming honesty, J.D. offers an insightful look at the spiritual realities which face us today. I love the section on 'Your New Identity'! Perhaps the most poignant and central truth for me is 'being gospel centered is not moving past the gospel but continually swimming deeper into it.' I encourage you to read this book."

—Dr. Frank Page, chairman of the Executive Committee of the
Southern Baptist Convention

"J.D. Greear is one of the greatest men of God I know. And one of the most brilliant. His ability to communicate the gospel in a fresh yet faithful way perfectly positions him to speak the life-giving message of Jesus into you in a way that you have never experienced. And in a way that will change your life forever."

—Steven Furtick, lead pastor, Elevation Church
and author of *Sun Stand Still*

"I've lived long enough to know that there's only one hope, one thing that can actually heal us and transform us: the grace-saturated gospel of Jesus. J.D. Greear invites us to dive into the bottomless end of the gospel pool and find life that deeply satisfies."

—Jud Wilhite, senior pastor of Central Christian Church,
Las Vegas and author of *Torn*,

"What is left if the gospel is lost? That question should haunt the evangelical mind as we are now surrounded by so many false Gospels, partial Gospels, and confused Gospels. Addressing this emergency, J.D. Greear offers sound counsel, clear biblical thinking, and the full measure of conviction in helping Christians and churches recover the authentic gospel of Jesus Christ."

—Dr. R. Albert Mohler Jr., president,
the Southern Baptist Theological Seminary
and author of *He Is Not Silent*

"The gospel truly changes everything. In *Gospel* Pastor J.D. Greear makes that truth crystal clear. In this book you will learn that Christ's presence and approval are all you need today and always for everlasting joy. I love this book for the blessing it will be to the body of Christ. It has a word for us all."

—Daniel L. Akin, president,
Southeastern Baptist Theological Seminary
and author of *Engaging Exposition*

"I believe God had J.D. write this book for such a time as this, for there has never been a time in the church where we so desperately needed to see the gospel more clearly, and the person of Christ so central to the gospel. This book is a gift from God to His church and to the world."

—Clayton King, president of Crossroads Worldwide
and author of *Dying to Live*

"If you're not amazed by the blood-soaked good news that ripped you from the grave, then you just might be on your way to being bored to death. And boredom leads to the futility of rote performance, pretending, and ultimately despair. I'm thankful one of my favorite preachers in the world, J.D. Greear, takes all that on in this book. With precision and punch, J.D. brings the shock and awe of gospel power. This book won't just engage your mind, it'll quicken your pulse."

—Russell Moore, dean of the School of Theology and senior vice-president for Academic Administration at the Southern Baptist Theological Seminary and author of *Adopted for Life*

I have spent my entire life studying movements. Great spiritual movements like Great Awakenings or missionary movements have at their center the recovery of the gospel. We desperately need such a movement in our time, and I for one believe we are seeing it. J.D. Greear gives clarity and perspective to this growing gospel movement. This book should be read by every person breathing, whether believer or not, whether "leader" or not. Get to know afresh the God who saves by reading this book, and find rescue for your soul.

—Alvin L. Reid, professor of Evangelism and Student Ministry,
Bailey Smith Chair of Evangelism at
Southeastern Baptist Theological Seminary

"Nothing has affected my life more than the gospel. My thirty-five years of pastoral ministry have given me an ever-increasing love for, and deeper awe of, its power. Dr. Greear has much to offer the body of Christ in embracing this gospel in all its glory. The gospel really is the power of God for salvation, so read and be forever reminded!"

—Johnny Hunt, senior pastor,
First Baptist Church of Woodstock

"I love the gospel and the way that the gospel fuels zeal . . . and I love the way that J.D. writes about it. This is a gospel saturated book that will guide you in your desire to love the Lord and your neighbor. I highly recommend it."

—Elyse Fitzpatrick, author of *Give Them Grace: Dazzling Your Kids with the Love of Jesus*

"With the clarity and conviction of a prophet, J.D. Greear calls us to more than accuracy and academics with the text. In his book he challenges us to be sure that the gospel is more than central to our theology . . . but that it has transformed our lives."

—Mac Brunson, senior pastor,
First Baptist Church of Jacksonville

"Are you tired of the disconnect between head-religion and heart-religion? Read this book. Are you tired of the treadmill of performance-driven Christianity? Read this book. Are you unclear about how your love for the gospel should play-out in your daily walk with God? Read this book. Are you tired of the empty 'gospel-jargon' that, regrettably, has become vogue in our day? Read this book. In this short volume, J.D. Greear has gifted the church with something wonderful: he calls us to rediscover the Source of the transforming power of the Christian life. In short, he beckons us, woos us, and drives us to Christ, our great treasure and eternal joy. Hopeful and life-giving, I highly recommend this book."

—Scott Anderson, executive director, Desiring God,
Minneapolis, Minnesota

"The fruit we crave—joy, peace, love, goodness—persistently eludes our techniques and formulae. J.D. Greear reminds us that Jesus and his gospel are both the means and the end. Savor this book."

—Glenn Lucke, president, Docent Research Group

GOSPEL

JD GREEAR

PUBLISHING GROUP

Nashville, Tennessee

Dedicated to the members of the Summit Church,
who have patiently walked with a pastor who was
rediscovering the revolutionary power of the gospel.

Against the world; for the world.
—St. Athanasius

Acknowledgments

To my wife, who has lived out the gospel as well as anyone I know. Her passionate love for Jesus has often rebuked my tendency toward separating knowledge from passion. Thank you for your patience with me, and for extending to me the grace of the gospel. In her grace I have seen that I am "first, sinner; only second, sinned against."

To my parents, who faithfully modeled a love for Jesus for the twenty years I spent in their home. They never used the term "gospel-centered," but they lived in awe of the God of gospel. That, as I see it, is the whole point of gospel-centeredness.

To Tim Keller, whose thinking has so permeated my own that I can no longer really tell where his stops and mine starts. I am heavily indebted to him for many of the ideas in this book, particularly in chapters 2, 3, and 6. I have listened to and read Tim Keller so much that I tend to plagiarize his interpretation of a passage before I even hear him teach on that passage. I told him that once, and he laughed and said he did the same thing with Ed Clowney. I have met Dr. Keller only twice, for a combined total of six minutes. The second time we met, I asked if I could call him my friend. He said yes. So, to my BFF Tim Keller, thank you. I have tried to note where I recount a point I heard from him. However, having listened to and read so much of his teaching, I sometimes forget when I heard something from him first. Any omission of citation is accidental.

To Paul Carlisle, Sam Williams, David Powlison, Elyse Fitzpatrick, and Ed Welch, whose counseling and writing have profoundly influenced my thinking. Since my first counseling class in seminary, I've always said that if I could preach like anyone, I'd preach like a counselor.

To my friends Bruce Ashford, Danny Akin, Mark Driscoll, Tyler Jones, Clayton King, Steven Furtick, David Platt, and Tullian Tchividjian: Hearing your insights, listening to you preach, and bouncing ideas off of you have changed the character of my ministry forever. You have been gifts of God to me.

Finally, I want to thank the loyal, patient team at B&H Publishing Group, particularly Jedidiah Coppenger, Michael Kelley, and Tom Walters for hours and hours of labor with me on this project. At times it seemed you were even more committed to this book than I was! Thank you for your dedication to making theologically rigorous material accessible to all. This book is much better because of your labors.

I have no desire at all to be original. I have had only three original thoughts in my lifetime, and they weren't that good. I desire for people to understand the concepts that are in this book. Consider me, and this book, merely a rehash of truths that God revealed to His people in ancient times. God is the source; the church is the conduit. I stand in grateful debt to both.

Contents

Part 3: Toward a Gospel-Centered
Understanding of Life

Foreword

BY TIMOTHY KELLER

One of the most startling passages in the Bible connects the magnificence of angels with the mystery of the gospel. Angels are incredibly majestic and powerful beings, living in God's eternal presence. Yet there is something that has happened on the earth that is so stupendous that even these immortal beings experience the persistent longing "to look into these things" (1 Pet. 1:12 NIV). What are "these things" that could possibly and consistently consume the attention of God-fixated creatures? The answer is—the gospel.

> Concerning this salvation, the prophets, who spoke of the grace that was to come to you, searched intently and with the greatest care. . . . It was revealed to them that they were not serving themselves but you, when they spoke of the things that have now been told you by those who have preached the gospel to you by the Holy Spirit sent from heaven. Even angels long to look into these things. (1 Pet. 1:10, 12 NIV)

The angels never get tired of looking into the gospel. This means that there is no end to gospel exploration. There are depths in the gospel that are always there to be discovered and applied not only to our ministry and daily Christian life, but above all to the worship of the God of the gospel with renewed vision and humility.

The underlying conviction in my preaching, pastoring, and writing is that the gospel—this eternally fascinating message craved by the angels—can change a heart, a community, and the world when it is recovered and applied. The gospel is life giving, because it generates changes that are received only by grace through faith. This foundational truth, however, gets bypassed, obscured, and forgotten, because, as Martin Luther noted, religion forms the default mode of the human heart. It is essential, then, that we distinguish religion from the gospel. Religion, as the default mode of our thinking and practices, is based upon performance: "I obey; therefore, I am accepted by God." The basic operating principle of the gospel, however, is, not surprisingly, an about-face, one of unmerited acceptance: "I am accepted by God through Christ; therefore, I obey." To truly understand this paradigm shift at a life-altering level requires that the gospel be explored and "looked into" at every opportunity and in regular, systematic ways.

When the gospel is explored in this way, it produces uncommon properties. Blaise Pascal, writing in the seventeenth century, reveals how this occurs:

> *Without this divine knowledge, how could we help feeling either exalted or dejected? The Christian religion alone has been able to cure these twin vices, not by using the*

one to expel the other according to worldly wisdom, but by expelling both through the simplicity of the gospel. For it teaches the righteous that they still bear the source of all corruption which exposes them throughout their lives to error, misery, death, and sin; and [yet] it cries out to the most ungodly that they are capable of the grace of the Redeemer. Thus, making those whom it justifies to tremble, yet consoling those whom it condemns, it so nicely tempers fear with hope through this dual capacity. . . . Grace and sin! It causes infinitely more dejection than mere reason—but without despair, and infinitely more exaltation than natural pride—but without puffing us up! (Pensées 208)

It is one thing to understand the gospel but is quite another to *experience* the gospel in such a way that it fundamentally changes us and becomes the source of our identity and security. It is one thing to grasp the essence of the gospel but quite another to think out its implications for all of life. We all struggle to explore the mysteries of the gospel on a regular basis and to allow its message to influence our thinking.

My fellow pastor, J.D. Greear, through his book, has helped us in this quest for gospel-saturated living. He takes the principles of gospel centrality and shows us how to orient our lives around it. I appreciate how in refreshing and real ways he makes the gospel accessible to others so that they can experience its transforming power. I especially like the book's practical section on gospel prayer as a way to assist us in rehearsing these truths deep into our hearts and minds.

Whether you are exploring Christianity for the first time or are longing to "look into these things" again and again, let me invite you to spend time with this helpful book.

Introduction

I am a professional Christian. But for many years I found Christianity to be wearisome. That's a confession you won't often hear from a pastor, but it was true of me.

I first put faith in Christ when I was in high school. My conversion, as far as I can tell, was sincere. I understood that Christ had paid the full penalty for my sin, and I surrendered to do whatever God wanted me to do. I got a big list of stuff to start and stop doing for God.

I went to a Christian school that emphasized conformity to a set of rules. We didn't dance, because dancing would make you have impure thoughts. And we couldn't listen to music with a beat in it because that would make you want to dance. We weren't allowed to go to see movies, because movies would make you worldly. We couldn't even go see the Christian movies when they came to the theater because if people saw us at the movies they might assume we were there to see worldly movies, and that might make them think it was *OK* for them to see worldly movies. It was rules like these that real Christians lived by.

I learned that real Christians tell other people about Jesus, so I set goals for how many people I would tell about Jesus in a given month. I even established a maximum time limit (fifteen minutes) for how long I would sit with a stranger on an airplane before bringing up whether or not they knew Jesus.

In college I learned that real Christians love international missions, so I took lots of mission trips (twenty-five countries in ten years!) and gave lots of money to missions. I even packed up my entire life into an oversized duffel bag and went to live in a third-world fundamentalist Muslim country for two years.

I later learned that real Christians love the poor. So I sponsored a Compassion child. But wasn't she just one in an endless sea of hurting people that desperately needed my help? Should I adopt five more? Twenty-five more? Did I really need to drink that Coke with dinner? Couldn't that money be used to feed another orphan? I constantly felt guilty about anything I owned. Whatever I gave, it wasn't enough, because there was *always* more I could give. And, after all, "God doesn't judge your giving by the amount you give, but by the amount you have left." I always had a little more left than the kid in India did.

And then of course, there was the unfortunate day that I read the biography of a missionary who talked about how much more you could do for God if you were single, and so I concluded if I was really serious about being used maximally for God, I had to be single. That's what Paul said, right? To paraphrase 1 Corinthians 7, he said, "I wish you were all like I am" (i.e., single), so you could be unencumbered in ministry. Thus, if I wanted my life to be *maximally* leveraged for God's kingdom, how could I desire anything *but* celibacy? Wouldn't I be willing to be single for seventy years so souls could be saved for eternity? So I tried to ignore girls for a semester during college—but to my chagrin, they wouldn't leave me alone. (At least that's how I remember it.)

By that time I was living in a way that would have met just about anybody's standard as a "real," committed Christian. But this religion of so-called grace often felt more to me like drudgery than delight. No matter how many rules I kept and how disciplined my life was, I walked around with an ever-present sense of guilt. In the deepest part of my heart, I knew—*knew*—God was not really pleased with me, because there was always something I could be doing better. The really good Christians were always doing something that I wasn't.

To make matters worse, my marriage kept revealing how selfish and petty I was. Seeing others more successful than me in ministry made me jealous to the point that I delighted in the thought of them falling into sin and being disqualified from ministry. I still felt enslaved to the lusts of my flesh. My service for God was fervent, but my passions for Him were cold. I certainly didn't *desire* to know Him more.

I was tired, and while I would never admit it, I was starting to hate God.

He was the merciless taskmaster always standing over me yelling, "NOT ENOUGH! I want MORE!" He was always there, waving damnation in my face, saying, "If you want My approval, there's something else you must *do*." His constant demands were driving me insane. The more I strived to walk in His ways, the less love I felt for Him. The more closely my feet followed Him, the more my heart ran away.

Oh, I had the facts down. I knew He had taken the penalty for my sin. I also knew that He was the universe's most satisfying possession. But if my head knew that truth, my heart didn't *feel* it. I was motivated to walk with God primarily by my desire to stay out of hell.

> The more closely my feet followed Him, the more my heart ran away.

Recently, however, I discovered something that has changed everything.

The gospel.

I know saying that sounds strange for an evangelical pastor who is leading a growing megachurch to say, but it is true.

It's not that I didn't understand or believe the gospel before. I did. But the truth of the gospel hadn't moved from my mind to my heart. There was a huge gap between my intellect and my emotions. The Puritan Jonathan Edwards likened his reawakening to the gospel to a man who had known, in his head, that honey was sweet, but for the first time had that sweetness burst alive in his mouth. That is what happened to me.

> The Puritan Jonathan Edwards likened his reawakening to the gospel to a man who had known, in his head, that honey was sweet, but for the first time had that sweetness burst alive in his mouth.

"Rediscovering" the gospel has given me a joy in God I never experienced in all my years of fervent religion. Now I sense, almost daily, a love for God growing in my heart, displacing a love for myself. The jealously that once consumed my heart is being replaced by a desire to see others prosper. I feel self-ishness giving way to tenderness and generosity. My cravings for the lusts of the flesh are being replaced by a craving for righteousness, and my self-centered dreams are being replaced by God-glorifying ambitions. A power is surging in me that is changing me and pushing me out into the world to leverage my life for the kingdom of God.

I still have a long way to go, and I daily have to struggle against the God-hating desires of my flesh, but I am changing. I am, as Paul would say, making "progress" in the gospel. The gospel has done in my heart what religion never could.

I believe it can do the same thing for you. That's what this book is about.

> *"Rediscovering" the gospel has given me a joy in God I never experienced in all my years of fervent religion.*

Over the next several chapters, I want to reacquaint you with the gospel. Not just with the doctrines, but with its power. The gospel is the announcement that God has reconciled us to Himself by sending His Son Jesus to die as a substitute for our sins, and that all who repent and believe have eternal life in Him. I want you to see the gospel not only as the means by which you get into heaven, but as the driving force behind every single moment of your life. I want to help, in some small way, your eyes to be opened (again) to the beauty and greatness of God. I want you to see how the gospel, and it alone, can make you genuinely passionate for God, free you from captivity to sin, and move you outward to joyful sacrifice on behalf of others.

Here's how we're going to go about this together. The
first section of this book is about *why* the gospel—and only
the gospel—is the means by which we can truly be changed.
I want to show you why "religious" (what we're going to call
"mechanical") change absolutely, positively, does not work. In
this section, I will show you how the gospel changes us in a
fundamentally different way than religion does, and that it can
do something in our hearts that religion is utterly unable to do.

In part 2 I want to introduce you to a simple tool that
has helped me, for several years now, saturate myself in the
gospel. It is a small, four-part prayer that I've come to call
"The Gospel Prayer." Each part of that prayer serves a specific
purpose, pointing you to what God has done for you in Christ
and how that changes how you see God, yourself, and others.
I believe this prayer can be the means by which you "preach
the gospel" to yourself daily.

As you read the first two sections, there will probably be
some questions that arise. Things like, "If we are free in Christ,
why do I still find so many commands in the Bible?" "What
should I do when I don't desire God?" "How much does God
expect me to do for Him?" "What does a true, gospel-centered
church look like?" and so forth. In the third section, I want to
confront these questions head on, and I hope to provide solid,
biblical answers for you. I hope this section will convince you
that the gospel really is, as the apostle Peter would say, all that
you need for life and godliness (2 Pet. 1:3).

That's it. Simple enough? Good. Time is wasting, and
the most amazing news in all the universe is waiting to be
discovered.

PART 1

How the Gospel Does What Religion Cannot

CHAPTER 1

The Missing Gospel

Is the gospel really missing? If so, where did it go?

Most Christians have the facts straight: Jesus was born of a virgin, lived a perfect life, died on the cross in our place, and was raised from the dead. All those who place their faith in Him will be forgiven and have everlasting life. So, the gospel is not missing.

Not so fast.

I mentioned in the introduction that there is a difference in knowing that honey is sweet and having that sweetness burst alive in your mouth. Being able to articulate the gospel with accuracy is one thing; having its truth captivate your soul is quite another.

The gospel is not just supposed to be our ticket into heaven; it is to be an entirely new basis for how we relate to God, ourselves, and others. It is to be the source from which everything else flows.

> *Being able to articulate the gospel with accuracy is one thing; having its truth captivate your soul is quite another.*

Let me lay all my cards on the table: I believe evangelicalism, as a whole, desperately needs a recovery of the gospel as the center of Christianity. Even in conservative denominations like my own (the Southern Baptist Convention), the gospel has been eclipsed by any number of secondary stimuli for growth.

I don't mean that we have corrupted the gospel—no, we've still got those facts right. But the goal of the gospel is not just that we pass some kind of test by accurately recounting the importance of Jesus. The goal of the gospel is to produce a type of people consumed with passion for God and love for others. We certainly don't seem to have *that* right.

A Christianity that does not have as its primary focus the deepening of passions for God is a false Christianity, no matter how zealously it seeks conversions or how forcefully it advocates righteous behavior. Being converted to Jesus is not just about learning to obey some rules. Being converted to Jesus is learning to so adore God that we would gladly renounce everything we have to follow Him.

In graduate school my roommate kept a dog named Max in our house. Because poor Max was crippled in his back legs, his life consisted of lying on our doorstep and staring up at us when we walked by. I remember looking at him one day and thinking, "Based on how most people see Christianity, Max would make a fine Christian: he doesn't drink; he doesn't smoke; he doesn't cuss; he doesn't get angry; we've had him neutered so his thought-life is under control."

Jesus' disciples are not supposed to be merely compliant, neutered dogs. Jesus' followers are to be *alive* with a love for God. When you love God and love others, Jesus said, all the rest of the Christian life falls naturally into place (Matt. 22:37–39).

> A *Christianity that does not have as its primary focus the deepening of passions for God is a false Christianity, no matter how zealously it seeks conversions or how forcefully it advocates righteous behavior.*

How Do We Learn to Love God?

How, then, do we learn to *love* God? That's the dilemma of the "great commandment": "You shall love the Lord your God with all your heart and with all your soul and with all your mind" (Matt. 22:37). But how can true love be *commanded*?

Being commanded to love someone you have no natural affection for becomes wearisome. True love grows as a response to loveliness. The first time I saw my wife, I felt the beginnings of love for her. The more I've gotten to know her over the years, and the more I've seen of her beauty, the more I've grown to love her. My love is a response.

Love for God is commanded in Scripture, but the command can only truly be fulfilled as our eyes are opened to see God's beauty revealed in the gospel. The Spirit of God uses the beauty of the gospel to awaken in our hearts a desire for God. "We love Him," the apostle John would say, "because

He first loved us" (1 John 4:19 NKJV). Love for God grows out of an experience of the love of God.

When we focus primarily on behavior change, we are ignoring the real issue: a heart that doesn't want to love God. That's certainly not to say that we should only obey God when we feel like it; only that preaching Christianity primarily as a set of new behaviors will create people who act right without ever loving the right.[1] This creates hypocrites, weary and resentful of God.

> Love for God grows out of an experience of the love of God.

What Is "Real" Spiritual Growth?

In the last message Jesus gave to His disciples, He told them that the way to fruitfulness and joy—the "secret" to the Christian life—was to *abide* in Him. They wouldn't produce "abundant fruit" by reading books, intensifying their self-discipline, memorizing Scripture, or getting in accountability groups. Those things all have their place, but real fruit comes only from one place: abiding in Jesus.

"Abiding in Jesus" may sound like spiritual mumbo jumbo to you. It always did to me. I assumed that when you were "abiding in Jesus" you'd walk around with an ethereal glow in your eye and inexplicably wake up at 4 a.m. strumming passion tunes on the golden harp you keep beside your bed. But the word *abide* is much more straightforward than that. The Greek word *meno* means literally "to make your home in." When we "make our home in" His love—feeling it, saturating ourselves with it, reflecting on it, standing in awe of it—spiritual fruit begins to spring up naturally from us like roses on a rosebush.

Spiritual "fruit," you see, is produced in the same way physical "fruit" is. When a man and woman conceive physical "fruit" (i.e., a child), they are usually not thinking about the mechanics of making that child. Rather, they get caught up in a moment of loving intimacy with one another, and the *fruit* of that loving intimacy is a child.

In the same way, spiritual fruit isn't made by focusing on the commands of spiritual growth.

> When we "make our home in" His love, spiritual fruit begins to spring up naturally from us.

You can't just grit your teeth and say, "I will have more loving feelings toward God! I will be more patient! I will have self-control!" I'll explain later the role for denial of the flesh and self-disciplines, but true spiritual *fruit* comes from getting swept up in intimate, loving encounters with Jesus Christ. His love is the soil in which all the fruits of the Spirit grow. When our roots abide *there*, then joy, peace, patience, kindness, gentleness, and self-control grow naturally in our hearts.

So if you want to see spiritual fruit in your life, don't focus primarily on the fruits. Focus on Jesus' acceptance of you, given to you as a gift. Focusing on spiritual fruit will usually produce only frustration and despair, not fruitfulness.

Have you ever looked at your life and thought, "Why am I still so impatient? How could I really be saved and still have such a problem with self-control?" I certainly have. If anything, the more I've walked with Jesus the more aware I've become of my sinfulness. Jesus, however, did not tell me to "abide" in my fruitfulness. He told me to abide in Him—in His acceptance of me, given to me freely as a gift.

Abiding in Jesus means understanding that His acceptance of us is the same regardless of the amount of spiritual fruit we have produced. Ironically, it is only when we understand that His love is not conditioned on our spiritual fruitfulness that we gain the power to become truly fruitful. Only those who abide in Him produce much fruit. In other words, those people who get better are those who understand that God's approval of them is not dependent on their getting better.

> *To see spiritual fruit in your life, don't focus primarily on the fruits. Focus on Jesus' acceptance of you, given to you as a gift.*

So what I really want to help you do in this book is abide in Jesus. The by-product of abiding in Jesus is that you will become more patient in your marriage; you will develop self-discipline; you will become generous. Abiding in Jesus will produce *all* of the fruits of the Spirit in you—but not by having you concentrate particularly on any of those things. You concentrate on Jesus. You rest in His love and acceptance, given to you not because of what you have earned, but because of what He has earned for you.

Without Love, It's Ultimately Worthless

My senior year of high school, I started a relationship with an incredible girl for whom I *should* have been head over heels. "On paper" she was perfect. The problem was that when we were together there was just no *magic*, if you know what I mean. I couldn't find a reason to *quit* dating her, however, so we kept on dating, even after I left for college 1,200 miles away.

I returned home for the first time over Christmas break, and we agreed to see each other the day before Christmas. All was well and good until the afternoon before I went to her house, when I had an alarming thought: *Was I supposed to get her a Christmas present?* It was, after all, the day before Christmas. If she got me a Christmas present and I didn't get her one, then I would look like a total sleezeball.

Just to be safe, I stopped at the mall on my way to see her. I went into a sporting goods shop, the natural place you look for romantic gifts, and there I saw it—the absolutely perfect gift: an Adidas snow-skiing neck-warmer. It was $7. I wrapped up the woolen masterpiece and put it under the seat in my car and drove the forty-five minutes over to her house. She came to the door, and after a few pleasantries, she said, "I bought you a Christmas present." I said, proudly, "I got you one too!" She said, "Here is yours!" and gave me a *beautifully* wrapped box from under the tree. I opened it and took out; to my horror, it was obviously a very expensive shirt.

She looked at me expectantly and said, "Where's my gift?"

I said, "Uhhh . . . I left it at home!" (Thinking that was safe . . . I could go home later, buy a new gift, and mail it to her. And I got to keep the neck-warmer. Win-Win.) But then she said, "Well, we don't have anything to do tonight. Maybe we could go back to your house and get it. I'd like to see your parents, anyway."

I'm sure that during the forty-five-minute drive home I seemed a little distant. It's because I was plotting. Praying. Vowing. When we walked in the house, I pulled my mom aside and said, "Hey—is there anything you were planning to give my sister that she doesn't know about yet?" My mom said, "Why?" I said, "No further questions, please." My mom went and got a gift intended for my sister (another pretty expensive sweater) and we put my date's name on it instead. I took it in to my "girlfriend" and said, confidently, "Here's your gift. I thought this would be perfect for you."

I've often wondered in the years since then what would have happened that night had I come clean and told her the truth that my gift to her was only done to save face. No doubt, she would have refused it flatly. No girl wants to be loved only out of obligation.

Somehow we think God is different, as if He is pleased when we serve Him because we're required to. He's not.

God desires a people who desire Him, who serve Him because they love Him. He "seeks those," Jesus said, "who worship Him in Spirit and in truth."

In fact, Paul says whatever we do for God that is not fueled by love for God is ultimately worthless to Him:

> *If I speak in the tongues of men and of angels, but have not love, I am a noisy gong or a clanging cymbal. And if I have prophetic powers, and understand all mysteries and all knowledge, and if I have all faith, so as to remove*

*mountains, but have not love, I am nothing. If I give
away all I have, and if I deliver up my body to be burned,
but have not love, I gain nothing. (1 Cor. 13:1–3)*

Let's face it: Paul's list here is impressive by anyone's
standard. "Speaking with the tongues of men and angels" has
to put you in the top 1 percent of spiritually gifted people.
"Understanding all mysteries and all knowledge" means that
you've got even the finer points of Christian doctrine down
pat. "Faith to remove mountains" means you can flat get stuff
done in prayer. And *"giving away even your body to be burned"*?
Wow. Obedience doesn't get any more "radical" than that.
When the offering plate goes by, you pull out a match and
light yourself on fire for God. That's Varsity.

Yet, Paul says, spiritual giftedness, doctrinal mastery,
audacious faith, and radical obedience *do not equal* the only
thing that actually *matters* to God—love for Him. Without
love even the most radical
devotion to God is of no
value to Him.

*Let me make sure that
sinks in . . .* You can gain
all the spiritual gifts in
the world. You can take
the most radical steps of
obedience. You can share
every meal with the home-
less in your city. You can
memorize the book of Leviticus. You can pray each morning
for four hours like Martin Luther. But if what you do does

> Spiritual giftedness,
> doctrinal mastery,
> audacious faith, and
> radical obedience do
> not equal *the only thing
> that actually* matters *to
> God—love for Him.*

not flow out of a heart of love—a heart that does those things because it genuinely *desires* to do them—it is ultimately *worthless* to God.

The point is that to produce *real* love in your heart for God takes something beyond spiritual gifts, greater doctrinal knowledge, audacious faith, and even radical obedience. Something entirely different. Radically different.

That's where the gospel comes in. The gospel, and the gospel alone, has the power to produce love for God in the heart. Paul calls the gospel "God's power for salvation" (Rom. 1:16). There are only two things that Paul ever refers to as "the power of God." One is the gospel; the other is Christ Himself. As the story of the gospel is proclaimed, the Spirit Himself makes the heart come alive to see the glory and beauty of God revealed in it. Just as Jesus' command to the lame man to "get up and walk" had *in itself* the power to obey the command, so the story of Jesus' death and resurrection has *in itself* the power to make dead hearts new. As the gospel is believed, through the power of the spirit, our selfish, hardened hearts burst alive with righteous and godly passions.[2] As we behold the glory of God in the face of Christ, Paul says, we are transformed into glory (2 Cor. 3:18–4:14).

Religion, then, can tell you what to do—namely, to "love God with all your heart, soul and mind" and "to love your neighbor as yourself"; but the gospel alone gives you the power to do it.

The gospel produces not just obedience, you see, but a new kind of obedience[3]—an obedience that is powered by desire. An obedience that is both pleasing to God *and* delightful to you.

Now, one clarification: I'm not saying here that every sacrifice we're asked to make for God will be in and of itself *desirable*. The cross was not in and of itself desirable to Jesus. Hebrews 12:2, in fact, says that Jesus had to *endure* its pain, which means He had to submit His desires to God's will. But even the crucifying of His flesh was shrouded in joy for Him. The joy of what He was obtaining—the pleasure of God and eternity with us—was greater than the pain.

That's how God wants our obedience to be as well. When we pick up

> The gospel produces an obedience that is powered by desire.

our cross to follow Him, He wants even the pain of the cross to be shrouded in joy over what we are obtaining.

That kind of joy in Jesus cannot be produced in us by simple resolutions to obey. That kind of joy comes only from being saturated in the gospel.

Thus, if you are not where you should be spiritually, the answer is not simply to get busier for Jesus. It is not just to get more radical in your devotion to God. It's not only to seek greater spiritual gifts or even to learn more about the Bible. It is to make your home in God's love given to you as a gift in Christ.

That's what I mean when I say the gospel is missing. We have substituted all kinds of cosmetic changes for true heart change. We encourage people to pursue new and better spiritual gifts. We tell them to recover ancient devotional techniques. We try to beef them up on a particular doctrinal system, as if more correct facts will do the trick in itself.

We tell them to show audacious, mountain-moving faith in prayer. We tell them to get radically committed to the Great Commission. These things all have their place, but all we are doing is piling superficial changes onto a heart that doesn't really love God. *None* of those things can produce love for God. Only the gospel can. Without that, ultimately our changes are worthless.

I am a lazy yardman. To my wife's chagrin, I don't (willingly) plant flowers.[4] I don't fertilize. I pay someone else to cut the grass. All I care about, as it relates to the yard, is that I don't get complaint letters from my neighbors and I can see the tops of my kids' heads when they go outside. My wife, on the other hand, loves a plush, bright, neatly manicured lawn. One day she complained that our flower beds had too many weeds in them, and that I needed to do something about it. Now, there are two ways to kill weeds. You can get on your knees and spend several hours pulling them up by the roots. This is the correct way. Or, you can napalm them with weed killer. This is the lazy way. My way. So, multiple times each summer I blasted our flower beds with weed killer . . . and all our weeds died, just like the advertisement promised. And so did quite a few rose bushes that were caught in the line of fire. Beautiful, green vines with budding scarlet flowers were turned into tumbleweeds.

My wife, of course, complained about that too. In a Spirit-filled way, of course. So, let's say that to make her happy I had gone down to the florist and bought several dozen roses, brought them home, and began to staple them to the dead branches of the rosebushes. Would I have fixed anything? For a while, the dead rosebushes may have given the appearance of being alive, at least from a distance. But they would not really be alive, and I would not really be out of the doghouse.

Paul Tripp has said that most of the strategies for Christian growth amount merely to "rose-stapling techniques." Give away more money. Be more serious about your sin. Be more disciplined in your life. Read your Bible and have accountability partners. Go to a small group.

Spiritual disciplines have their place (we'll get to that later). But nothing can take the place of organic change in the heart.

Only in the gospel, you see, is the power to obey the first commandment. Only in the truths of the gospel can a heart turned in on itself burst alive in love for God.

For many evangelicals the gospel has functioned solely as the entry rite into Christianity; it is the prayer we pray to begin our relationship with Jesus; the diving board off of which we jump into the pool of Christianity. After we get into the pool, we get into the real stuff of Christianity: mastering good principles for our marriage; learning rules and regulations of how to behave; and figuring out if Kirk Cameron will be left behind.

The gospel, however, is not just the diving board off of which we jump into the pool of Christianity; it is the pool itself. It is not only the way we begin in Christ; it is the way we grow in Christ. As Tim Keller says, the gospel is not just the ABCs of Christianity, it is the A–Z; it is not the first step in a stairway of truths, it is more like the hub of God's wheel of truth.[5] All other Christian virtues flow out of it.

That's why growth in Christ is never going beyond the gospel, but going deeper into the gospel. The purest waters

> The gospel is not just the diving board off of which we jump into the pool of Christianity; it is the pool itself.

from the spring of life are found by digging deeper, not wider, into the gospel well.

My prayer is that this book will call us to a deeper understanding of the gospel as the true center of Christianity. I hope it helps you see that the gospel shouldn't just be a ticket to heaven but the core of our entire lives. When you have made your home in the gospel, you will be radically generous. You will show audacious faith. These things are not added after the gospel, they flow from the gospel.

The apostle Peter says that the angels still "long to look into" the things of the gospel, because it dazzles their minds (1 Pet. 1:12). The angels have seen God face-to-face, and yet they still can't get enough of the gospel! Do we think we are really ready to move on to something else?

Whatever spiritual dysfunction you have in your life, the cure is the gospel. Do we want to be filled with passion for God? We should drink from the gospel. Do we want to get control of our bodies? We must be captivated by the gospel. Do we want to be content with what we have? We need to feast on the gospel. Do we want to learn to love our spouse? We have to be overwhelmed by the gospel.

> Growth in Christ is never going beyond the gospel, but going deeper into the gospel.

Martin Luther said in his *Lectures on Romans* that true spiritual progress was "always to begin again." He said we must daily "embrace the love and kindness of God . . . and daily exercise our faith therein; entertaining no doubt of God's love and kindness."[6]

Always "begin again" with the gospel. Abide in it; swim in it; make your home in it. See more and more of your life through it. Be absolutely convinced at every moment of every day of the goodness of God in your life. That's the only way you'll ever *really* grow.

The gospel has done its work in us when we crave God more than we crave everything else in life—more than money, romance, family, health, fame—and when seeing His kingdom advance in the lives of others gives us more joy than anything we could own. When we see Jesus as greater than anything the world can offer, we'll gladly let everything else go to possess Him. When we love others like He loves us, we'll willingly yield our possessions to see His kingdom come into their lives.

> The gospel has done its work in us when we crave God more than we crave everything else in life.

Obedience that does not flow from love ends up being drudgery—both to us, and to God. The gospel turns that drudgery into delight. It changes us from being slaves who *have* to obey God to sons and daughters who *want* to obey God. Again, God is not just after obedience; He's after a whole new kind of obedience—an obedience that is filled with desire.

Dwelling on the riches of the gospel has forever changed my life. It has transformed our church. I believe with my whole heart it can change you too. But the humbling thing for me is that I can't really *teach* any of this to you. These things are spiritually revealed and spiritually discerned. They require the gift of heavenly eyes. I couldn't even teach it to myself when it was right in front of my face, so what would make me think I could illuminate your heart?

God is after an obedience that is filled with desire.

And what makes *you* think you can develop a passion for God by reading a book? So why not stop right now and plead with God to open the eyes of your heart? You might use the words of Paul in his prayer for the Ephesians,

> *[I pray] that the God of our Lord Jesus Christ, the Father of glory, may give you a spirit of wisdom and of revelation in the knowledge of him, having the eyes of your hearts enlightened . . . [and I pray that you] may have strength to comprehend with all the saints what is the breadth and length and height and depth, and to know the love of Christ that surpasses all knowledge, that you may be filled with all the fullness of God. (Eph. 1:17–18; 3:18–20)*

CHAPTER 2

Why Religious Change Doesn't Work

I walked out into our backyard one Saturday and encountered my four-year-old daughter, Kharis, pouring water from a watering can into her sandbox. When I asked what she was doing, she replied, without looking up, "Daddy, I need the sand to grow. See? There's not much left."

I tried to explain to her sand does not grow by watering it, because, of course, it is not alive. The only way to increase the amount of sand in the sandbox is for Daddy to pour more sand in.

That's how religion changes you. Religion pours it on. It gives you a lot of stuff "to do": Bible studies to go to; new habits to add to your life; things to say and not say, etc. That's what some have called "mechanical" change.[1]

That's fundamentally different from how a tree grows. A tree grows and bears fruit because it is alive. Fruits spring up naturally because of the life inside. This is how the gospel changes you. Your behavior changes because you change. This is an "organic" change.

Most strategies you hear for growth in Christ end up being, for all their Christian language, "mechanical" changes. We get busy for God. We add new spiritual disciplines. We give money. We do missions.

In the old days we even turned in an offering envelope that charted our spiritual busyness for the week. The envelope asked questions like:

- Have you read your Bible this week?
- Have you prayed?
- Have you shared your faith with someone this week?
- Is there a tithe/building fund/mission pledge contribution in this envelope?

It used to be a game to me to see if I could commence and complete all the elements on the envelope from the time the offering started to the time it got back to me. I shared Christ with my poor sister (who sat beside me in church) every week for a couple of years.

The problem with mechanical changes is that they quickly become wearisome to you. That's not to say you shouldn't ever do things when you don't want to do, just that if the extent of your Christianity is achieving the right behavioral standard, you are setting yourself up for disaster. You are laying religion onto a heart that loves other things. And, whether you ever articulate it or not, you will resent God holding you captive to do stuff you wouldn't otherwise be doing if He weren't threatening damnation.

The reason "mechanical" changes don't really work for us goes back to the core of what's wrong with us—all the way back to our original sin in the garden of Eden. I want to take us there in this chapter, because only then we can understand why religion won't work and why only the gospel can "fix" us.

> You will resent God holding you captive to do stuff you wouldn't otherwise be doing if He weren't threatening damnation.

Functional Gods

Our original sin was idolatry.[2] You may have a hard time seeing that. "Idolatry? I don't see them bowing down or praying to an idol." That's because we sometimes fail to grasp what worship really is. You worship whatever it is you deem most essential for life and happiness. For Adam and Eve it was the tree of the knowledge of good and evil. Its fruit was so important they were willing to disobey God to get it. For us, it may be money, the praise of others, a good marriage, a healthy family, achieving a certain status at work, or experiencing some sensual pleasure.

When something becomes so important to you that it drives your behavior and commands your emotions, you are worshipping it. You are willing to say "no" to God to get it.

The Hebrew word for "glory" (*kabod*) literally means "weight." To give something glory in your life (or, to worship it) is to give it so much weight that you couldn't imagine doing

life without it. An idol can be almost anything—even the good
gifts of God. Family, friends, dreams, even church—these
are all good things, of course. But they become idols when we
assign them "God-type"
weight.

> An idol can be almost
> anything—even the good
> gifts of God.

Ultimately, idolatry is
behind all of our sin. We
place a greater weight on
something other than God.
Whatever those things are
that we feel like we can't live without and that control our
behaviors are "functional gods" to us.[3] We may not prostrate
our bodies before them, but we prostrate our hearts.

All people, religious or not, have gods, because all are
worshippers. Many people feel like they are not worshippers
because they aren't religiously active. You can no more turn
off your drive for worship
by not being religious than
you could turn off your sex
drive by remaining single.
All human beings have
something they believe to
be essential for life; something that they could not

> All people, religious or
> not, have some sort
> of god, because all are
> worshippers.

imagine feeling happy or fulfilled without. Whatever, that
thing is, you are worshipping it, biblically speaking.

Functional Saviors

The first sensation Adam and Eve had after the thrill of eating the forbidden fruit was a sense of their own nakedness. Were they naked before eating the fruit? Yes. But only after they had eaten the fruit did their nakedness bother them. What had changed?

The early church fathers (guys like Gregory of Nazianzus and Athanasius) explained that prior to their sin Adam and Eve had been "clothed" in the love and acceptance of God, so their nakedness did not bother them. Now having stripped themselves of God's love and acceptance, they were left with a sense of exposure, fear, guilt, and shame.

So what did Adam and Eve do about that sense of nakedness? The same thing any of us do when we feel naked—they looked for something to put on! If you have a problem sleepwalking and suddenly woke up one night standing in a Super Walmart, buck naked, you probably wouldn't use that opportunity to pick up a few odds and ends you needed for the house. Instead, you'd immediately look for the clothing section and find something to cover yourself. And pray that no one you know has seen you.

Adam and Eve did essentially the same thing. They made themselves "coverings of fig leaves" and hid from God. Their clothes made them *feel* more acceptable.

We have all been on the same quest ever since. We try to cover the shame of our nakedness by establishing our worthiness in some way. We find something that sets us apart from others: we're smarter; we got into a certain kind of school; we have a good job and make lots of money; we're a good parent; we're more faithful in our religion than others. We'll use just about anything to establish our worth. People who aren't religious at all do this just as much as religious people. Atheists feel like they are fair-minded and good citizens. Hollywood stars pride themselves as social activists. Tony Soprano says, "I may kill lots of people . . . but I'm a good son." Everybody looks for things to justify their worthiness.

For most of us, life is like one big *Survivor* episode where we are trying to convince God and everyone else why we are not the ones who should be thrown off the island.

The things we use to establish our worthiness, can be called "functional saviors."

Why Religious Change Doesn't Work

Religious change, no matter how well-intentioned, doesn't work for three primary reasons:

1. Religious activities fail to address the "root" idolatries that drive our sin.

At its root, our sins are driven by the fact that we desire something more than we desire God. Religious change targets the acts of sin without addressing the idolatry that prompted that sin in the first place. In fact, a lot of times, religion becomes simply another way to get hold of that thing we most desire.

> *Religious change targets the acts of sin without addressing the idolatry that prompted that sin in the first place.*

Let me give you an example: Tim Keller tells of a notoriously sexually promiscuous kid he knew in college. The young man's sexual prowess was about more than lust, however. Gaining "notches on his bed post" was a source of identity to him—it proved he was a man, gained the admiration of his peers, and gave him a sense of power over women.

During his junior year this guy got involved with a campus ministry and "got saved." He quickly got "on fire for Jesus" and gave an inspiring, bold testimony of his new commitment to Christ.

However, Keller says, there was still something "off" about this guy. He was not a very enjoyable person to be around. If you were in a discussion with him, he had to show why he was right and you were wrong. In a small group he wanted you to recognize *his* opinions as insightful. He always wanted the positions of prominence.

The guy had all the external signs of love for Jesus. He had repented of his sexual promiscuity. He went to lots of Bible studies and witnessed boldly for Jesus. However, it was apparent that he had simply traded sex for religion as the outer manifestation of his true desire. What he really wanted—his "root idol"—was power over others.[4]

This is not conversion to Christ. This is a new means of pursuing an old idol.

True worship is obedience to God for no other reason than that you delight in God. There is a fundamental difference in serving God to get something from Him and serving Him to get more of Him. When I was in college, I had to take at least one course in fine arts to graduate.[5] I remember looking at my options and seeing something on classical music, something on poetry, and something on drama as my choices.

Nothing really sounded appealing, but I thought there was a chance that in the drama course we'd get divided up to do skits or something, and that sounded more enjoyable than sitting around listening to records or emoting poetry.

Mistake. Half of the course was spent learning the names of obscure French directors, and the other half watching videos of men in tights leap and prance about the stage. Every week I checked my man-card at the door before I walked into the class. But I needed a good grade in the course to maintain my GPA, so I toughed it out, studied hard, and managed to pull an A.

That was more than fifteen years ago. Since that time, a lot has changed. I have gotten married. I have three daughters. And my wife and I now have season tickets to our city's performing arts center, where we pay top dollar to see . . . *ahhemm* . . . theater. Men in tights prance about the stage. And I enjoy it. Not the tights part, but the other stuff.

Think about it—how thick is *that* irony? In college I used theater as a means to get money. I studied it hard so I could get a good grade so I could get a good job so I could *make money*. But now I use my hard-earned money to get more theater. Theater used to be the means to money, now it is the end of my money.

> True religion is when you serve God to get nothing else but more of God.

True religion is when you serve God to get nothing else but more of God. Many people use religion as a way of getting something else from God they want—blessings, rewards, even escape from judgment. This is wearisome to us, and to God. But when God is His own reward, Christianity becomes thrilling. Sacrifice becomes joy.

In other words, getting religiously active in a church, even in a good one, does not necessarily mean you have become a true *worshipper* of God. You may have simply dis-covered religion to be a more convenient means to other cherished idols like respect, pride, success, a good family, or prosperity.

> Getting religiously active in a church does not necessarily mean you have become a true worshipper *of God.*

2. When our acceptance is based on our performance, we exacerbate two root sins in our heart: pride and fear.

The exposure of our nakedness implanted in us a deep sense of fear. We sensed that we were not acceptable as we were (which is true), so we felt driven to do something to make ourselves more acceptable to God.

But whatever we think makes us better than others, we feel proud about, and that leads us to more sin. Pride gives rise to violence, impatience, intolerance, judgmentalism, and many other vices.

Of course, on the other hand, when we don't feel like we measure up to others, we despair. Our sense of nakedness and fear of rejection grows. This leads only to more fervent attempts to distinguish ourselves from others, and jealousy and hatred of those around us. Our despair creates a void that we often turn to the lusts of the flesh to fill. Despair over our soul "nakedness" drives people to crave drugs, alcohol, creature comforts, etc. It turns people into workaholics, serial romantics, and obsessive parents.

While performance-based acceptance thrusts us into a cycle of pride and despair, acceptance by God's grace produces exactly the opposite fruits. The assurance of God's presence and approval takes away our sense of nakedness and our craving for their approval. We are complete in Him. We are even free to let others see our faults, because we know we already have the absolute approval of the only One whose opinion really matters anyway. We become gracious and kind toward others, because we are aware of how much we've been forgiven. We are not afraid to lose all we have, because in Him we have all that we need.

> While performance-based acceptance thrusts us into a cycle of pride and despair, acceptance by God's grace produces exactly the opposite fruits.

The third reason religious change doesn't work has to do with its sustainability.

3. The insecurity of always wondering if we've done enough to be accepted causes resentment of God, not love for Him.

As I noted at the beginning of this book, when I first became a believer, I constantly felt guilty about things I needed to do better to become a good Christian. Despite my fervency, my love for God was not growing. Truth be told, I didn't want to get closer to God. He'd just point out something else

I should be doing before He'd approve of me. So I wanted to keep Him "paid off" and at a distance so I could be at peace. As Martin Luther, the great Reformer, noted about himself, my fear of God's judgment was producing a hatred for Him that was driving my heart farther and farther away from Him, even if my actions looked, on the surface, more godly.

That's because true love for God cannot grow when we are unsure about His feelings for us. All of our service for God will be done with an eye to elevating our status before Him. Ultimately, this is not love for God—it's love for ourselves. Charles Spurgeon told a story illustrating this:

> Once upon a time, a very poor carrot farmer lived on a small farm in rural England. During one harvesting season, he unearthed the largest carrot he had ever seen. He thought, "Now that is a carrot that befits a king." So he traveled to the king's palace, obtained an audience, laid the carrot joyfully at the king's feet. "Oh king," he said, "you have always been such a wonderful, fair and gracious king to me, and I love you very much. As a token of my love for you, I want you to have this carrot. It is a gift which you truly deserve." The king, touched by this man's simple offering, responded, "Thank you for this gift. I happen to own the farmland that surrounds your farm and I would like to give you that land as a gift. Please know that it also is a small token of the affection that I have for you, my son."
>
> One of the king's noblemen, standing in the court that day, thought, "Wow! If the king would give all

that farmland in response to a carrot, imagine what he would give for a real gift!" So the nobleman went that night and found the most majestic horse he'd ever seen and brought it to the king the next day. The crafty nobleman said, "King, you are a wonderful and worthy king. As a token of my love for you, I want you to have this horse as a gift."

The king, being very wise, saw through the ruse, and said to the nobleman, "Yesterday the poor man was giving the carrot to me. But today, you are giving the horse to yourself."[6]

When our salvation depends upon our righteous behavior, our righteousness will be driven by a desire to elevate ourselves in the eyes of God. This is not love for God; it's self-protection.

The gospel turns religion upside down. The gospel assures us of God's acceptance, given to us as a gift earned by Christ's worthiness, not ours. In response to that gift, we are moved to obey. Love for Him grows in response to His love for us.

> *True love for God cannot grow when we are unsure about His feelings for us.*

The British pastor D. Martyn Lloyd-Jones once asked his congregation what they would do if while they were away from home one day, a friend, who was at their home visiting, paid an overdue bill for them. "It depends on how much the bill was for," Lloyd-Jones said. If it were a small, unpaid postage on a

letter, you'd pat them on the back and say, "Thanks." If the
IRS had finally caught up to you after ten years of unpaid
taxes and had come to
take you to jail, and your
friend paid off your entire
debt, you would not pat
them on the back and say,
"Thanks." You would fall at their feet and say, *"Command me!"*

> The gospel turns religion
> upside down.

The gospel reawakens us to the beauty of God and
overwhelms us with mercy. Our behavior changes because
we change. Until that happens, all religious changes will be
superficial. Even if you force yourself to act right, your heart
will be going the other direction. This is the doctrine of total
depravity.

The Gospel According to J.D.

Let me explain how this plays out in my life. I have
certain sins I struggle with, but behind those sins are some
deeper sins that usually go unnoticed.

One night my wife and I decided to do some psycho-
analysis on me to determine what my most frequently recurring sins and dysfunctions were, and why I struggled so much
with them. (Note: I would
not advise doing this with
your spouse, unless you
have unusually thick skin.
From now on I'm doing
this *alone*.)

> The gospel reawakens
> us to the beauty of
> God and overwhelms
> us with mercy.

Anger. She pointed out that I get most angry when I either (a) feel like I'm losing an argument or (b) someone is making me look stupid. That is because, we determined, I need people to admire me, and I feel (however right or wrong) that my intelligence is a key component to gaining their respect. Behind my flashes of anger is an idolization of the admiration of others. I need the admiration of others in order to have happiness and value. The approval of others is my functional god and functional savior. God's presence and love are not sufficient for me.

Overwork and neglect of family. I overwork because I desperately want to be successful. And why do I need to be successful? Because I believe that if I'm successful that I'll have the approval of others.

Worry. Where does my worry come from? We determined that my worry usually arises from the fear that I'm not going to be the success that I want to be. The church is going to fail; I'm going to be a laughingstock; I'm going to only be mediocre. But, again, why do I need to be successful, to stand out from the crowd? Because I need to be admired by others.

Depression. When do I get depressed? It's usually after I preach a bad sermon. And it's not that I'm just frustrated that my people didn't get the message. I am devastated because my identity is built on my skill and reputation as a preacher. If I am a good preacher, then people will admire me.

Lying. The temptation for me to lie arises, my wife and I determined, from two places: (1) I lie to cover up my shortcomings and exaggerate my accomplishments. And why do I do that? You know the answer. (2) I lie to keep others happy because I don't want to disappoint them. Being a first-born, type A, people pleaser, I don't like to let people down. Because, if people are disappointed with me, then they are not approving of me, and we've already established that I can't handle that. My lying is symptomatic of my worship for people's approval.

You say, "J.D., you are one sick dude." I am. But so are you. I'm just brave enough to put it in print. (And, incidentally, maybe the reason I'm willing to do that is because I think that being so honest will make you admire me for my transparency. Ahh . . . it never ends!)

In any of these five sins, you can command me: *"J.D.! Don't be angry!"* Or, *"Thou shalt not lie!"* But you might as well tell a dog not to bark. My problem is that my heart so craves the approval of others that these sins come as instinctively to me as breathing!

My insecurity makes me fearful. It makes me be short-tempered. It makes me willing to bend the truth for personal advantage. And even if I could discipline myself not to get angry or worried or lie, I would have only covered up the real problem: I delight more in the approval of others than I do in the approval of God. I am an idolater. That is my depravity.

The "laws" of God (i.e., commands like, "J.D., don't lie, be depressed, worry, or get angry") tell me what to do, but don't really give me the power to do them—at least to obey them from the heart.

What religion is unable to do, God does for us in the gospel. The gospel shows me a God who is better than the approval of others and a God more valuable than their praise. The gospel shows me that God's presence and approval are the greatest treasure in the universe. The gospel reveals God's mercy toward me, and that makes me more merciful with others—not because I have to be so to gain God's accep-

> *The gospel shows me a God who is better than the approval of others and a God more valuable than their praise.*

tance, but because I am so overwhelmed by His mercy that I can't help but extend that to others.

We must saturate ourselves, therefore, in the truths of the gospel.

So, in the text that follows, I want to give you a tool to do just that. It's a prayer I've prayed every day for several years to immerse myself in the truths of the gospel. I simply call it, "The Gospel Prayer."

The Gospel Prayer

First, let me make sure you understand: there's nothing magical about this prayer. It's not an incantation to get God to do good things for you. Incidentally, it's also not my attempt to replace the Lord's Prayer. This prayer is simply a tool to help you train your mind in the patterns of the gospel. The point is not the prayer; the point is thinking in line with the gospel.

The Gospel Prayer has four parts. The first two parts lead us inward, helping us to renew our minds in God's acceptance of us and the value of that acceptance to us:

> *1. "In Christ, there is nothing I can do that would make You love me more, and nothing I have done that makes You love me less."*

2. *"Your presence and approval are all*
I need for everlasting joy."

Part 3 of the prayer has us consider what responding to the grace of the gospel looks like. Understanding God's generosity toward us should lead us to radical generosity toward others.

3. *"As You have been to me, so I will be to others."*

Part 4 of the prayer helps us see our world through the lens of the gospel and moves us to audacious faith. If the cross really does reveal God's compassion for sinners and the resurrection reveals His power to save them, then our prayers on their behalf should be audacious and bold:

4. *"As I pray, I'll measure Your compassion by the cross*
and Your power by the resurrection."

I've prayed this prayer every day now for the last few years. You know what? It's finally starting to sink in.

PART 2

The Gospel Prayer

The Gospel Prayer

*"In Christ, there is nothing I can do
that would make You love me more, and nothing
I have done that makes You love me less."*

*"Your presence and approval are all
I need for everlasting joy."*

"As You have been to me, so I will be to others."

*"As I pray, I'll measure Your compassion by the cross
and Your power by the resurrection."*

CHAPTER 3

The Gospel as Gift-Righteousness

How does God feel about you, right now? And how do you determine that? Do you base your answer on what kind of week you've had? How consistent your quiet times have been? Whether you've been nice to your children? For many years qualifications like these drove my response.

If I'd had a good week—a real "Christian" week"—I *felt* close to God. When Sunday came around, I would feel like lifting my head and hands in worship, almost as if to say, "God, here I am . . . I know You're excited about seeing me this week." If I'd had a stellar week, I loved being in God's presence and was sure God was pretty stoked about having me there too.

But the opposite was also true.

If I hadn't done a good job at being a real Christian, I felt pretty distant from God. If I'd fallen to some temptations, been a jerk to my wife, dodged some easy opportunities to share Christ, was stingy with my money, forgotten to recycle, kicked the dog, etc. . . . well, on those weeks I felt like God wanted nothing to do with me. When I came to church, I had no desire to lift my soul up to God. I was pretty sure He didn't want to see me either. I could *feel* His displeasure—His lack of approval.

That's because I didn't really understand the gospel. Or, at least I had forgotten it.

The Gospel

The gospel is that Christ has suffered the full wrath of God for my sin. Jesus Christ traded places with me, living the perfect life I should have lived, and dying the death I had been condemned to die. Second Corinthians 5:21 says that He actually *became* my sin so that I could literally *become* His righteousness. Saint Athanasius called this "the great exchange." He took my record, died for it, and offers me His perfect record in return. He took my shameful nakedness to clothe me with His righteousness. When I receive that grace in repentance and faith, full acceptance becomes mine. He lived in my place, and died in my place, and then offered to me a gift. Theologians call that "gift-righteousness."

> *God's righteousness has been given to me as a gift. He now sees me according to how Christ has lived, not on the basis of what kind of week I've had.*

That means that God could not love me any more than He does right now, because God could not love and accept Christ any more than He does, and God sees me in Christ. God's righteousness has been given to me as a gift. He now sees me according to how Christ has lived, not on the basis of what kind of week I've had.

Christ's salvation is 100 percent complete, and 100 percent the possession of those who have received it in repentance and faith. That's what we confess in the first part of The Gospel Prayer:

> *"In Christ, there is nothing I can do*
> *that would make You love me more, and nothing*
> *I have done that makes You love me less."*

Just let that sink in for a moment. Right now, if you are in Christ, when God looks at you—regardless of your situation—He sees the righteousness of Christ. If we really believed that—not only with our heads but also with our hearts—it would change everything in our lives.

> If you are in Christ, when God looks at you—regardless of your situation—He sees the righteousness of Christ.

A New Way of Approaching God . . . and Life

Imagine if you could say this to God: "God, here is why I think You should hear my prayer: this week, I concluded a forty-day fast, and during that time I met Satan in the flesh, stared him down, and resisted all his temptations. And then I suffered unjustly at the hand of sinners, but did so without complaint or the first flash of selfish anger. The only time I opened my mouth was to forgive those who were doing that to me. Also, I walked on water, healed a blind guy on the spot, and fed five thousand hungry men with a loaf of bread."

According to the gospel, *that is exactly what you can, and should, say.* Jesus' death has paid for every ounce of your sin; His perfect life has now been credited to you. In light of that, do you really feel like you could make God more favorable to you by doing your quiet time every day?

> *Christ's obedience is so spectacular there is nothing we could do to add to it; His death so final that nothing could take away from it.*

Christ's obedience is so spectacular there is nothing we could do to add to it; His death so final that nothing could take away from it.

Scripture says that we are not to come into the presence of God timidly or apprehensively but with "boldness" (Heb. 4:16 HCSB). The boldness that comes from knowing that God sees us according to the accomplishments of Christ.

For most of us, that is completely counterintuitive. Martin Luther said that our hearts are hardwired for "works-righteousness"—that is, the idea that what we do determines how God feels about us. Unless we are

> *Our hearts are hardwired for "works-righteousness."*

actively preaching the gospel to ourselves daily, we fall back into "works-righteousness."

Satan's A-game

Do you know who loves to push us to evaluate ourselves according to how well we've done? Our enemy, Satan. Satan, believe it or not, loves to convict us of our sins. That's one of his names—the "accuser of our brethren" (Rev. 12:10 NKJV). One of Satan's most effective weapons, I believe, is making us forget the identity the Father has declared over us in Christ and basing our sense of approval on how well we've done.

You can actually see that played out in the life of Jesus. When Satan tempted Jesus in the wilderness, he tried to redirect Jesus' attention from the Father's declaration on to other sources of validation (Matt. 4:1–7).

"[Since] you are the Son of God . . ."[1]

Embedded in that question is a doubt. The enemy was implying, "Well, since You are the 'Son of God,' Messiah boy . . . shouldn't You be able to make things different? Why would the 'Son of God' be out here in the desert all alone? Shouldn't You be able to make bread from the stones, or have the angels catch You when You fall?"

What was significant about that was the Father had just declared over Jesus in the previous chapter: "This is my beloved Son, with whom I am well pleased" (Matt. 3:17). Rather than feasting on the Father's declaration, the enemy wanted Him to look to other forms of validation for His divine Sonship. Jesus told the enemy that He did not need bread or protection to prove He was the Father's Son; the Father's declaration was sufficient.

If there were ever a time for Satan to bring out his "A-game," this would have been it. Don't you think it is sig-nificant that Satan began his "A-game" by trying to get Jesus to take His eyes off of the identity the Father had declared over Him and to seek valida-tion in other ways?

> *Satan's most effective weapon is to take our eyes off of what God has declared over us in the gospel.*

Satan's approach to us is the same. Satan's most effective weapon is to take our eyes off of what God has declared over us in the gospel.

Did you catch that?

Satan's primary temptation strategy is to try and make us forget what God has said about us and to evaluate our standing before God by some other criteria.

A lot of times when we think about spiritual warfare we think of it in terms of strange, paranormal phenomena—people levitating six feet above their beds, their eyes rolling in the back of their heads and foaming at the mouth, singing back-masked heavy metal music . . . Does Satan do stuff like that? I wouldn't put it beneath him. But I'm pretty confident that's not his main strategy.

He attacks our identity in the gospel. Satan's one direct shot at Jesus didn't include levitation or Ouija boards; nor did he show Jesus pornographic pictures out in the wilderness. He redirected Jesus' mind away from God's declaration over Him.

And his questions, of course, had a ring of truth in them. Why would God leave His Son alone in the desert?

Satan's questions always have a ring of truth in them. Our enemy, for example, will correctly point out our failures. Sometimes he helps us see how badly we're doing at being a Christian by showing us someone who is a much better Christian than we are: *"Wow—did you hear how much Scripture that guy knows? That's what a real Christian sounds like. But you? Your Bible knowledge is pathetic."*

Other times he puffs us up with pride: *"At least you don't struggle with jealousy like she does."* Either strategy is effective, because in either case we take our focus off of Christ's gift-righteousness and put it onto ourselves. And comparison with others leads to two of Satan's favorite sins: pride and despair. Pride leads to hardness of heart toward God and hatred of others. Despair leads us to depression, fear, and indulgence in the lusts of the flesh. This is the cycle he loves to have us in. Both start with unbelief of the gospel.

When Satan takes our eyes off of the declaration spoken over us at the gospel, we lose the security and satisfaction we have in the loving approval of our heavenly Father. The gateway is then opened for all the other temptations.

Jesus responded to these temptations by speaking confidently of the Father's approval of Him. Jesus put faith in God's word. He

> *When Satan takes our eyes off of the declaration spoken over us at the gospel, we lose the security and satisfaction we have in the loving approval of our heavenly Father.*

maintained His "beloved Sonship" even in the face of great trial and doubt. We will overcome the enemy in the same way.

So get this clearly: both Satan and the Holy Spirit will point out your sin. But they do so in entirely different ways and for entirely different purposes. I've heard it said like this:

> Satan starts with what you did, and tears down who you are. The Holy Spirit starts with what Christ has declared over you, and helps you rebuild what you did.[2]

Satan beats us down with our failures. Jesus calls us up into our identity. Jesus starts with the perfect state He has purchased for us by His death and uses the power of His resurrection to bring us into conformity with it.

Each day Jesus says to us, "You are My beloved child. I am well pleased in you. Now live that way." Satan, on the other hand, says, "Look at you. Look at the condition of your circumstances. Look at how poorly you're living. There is no way you are God's beloved child." Which voice are you going to believe? There's an eternity of difference between them.

When my oldest daughter, Kharis, was six years old, she was very timid, and I couldn't get her to try anything new—new foods, new playgrounds, rides at the fair, skydiving, bear hunting, cave spelunking—none of it! I'd encourage her to try something and she'd say, "I'm scared, Daddy. I don't want to." I talked to her several times about the need to be brave. One day she and my four-year-old daughter, Allie, and I were riding in the car and talking about the state fair coming to town. I said, "Maybe this year, Kharis, we can do the

Ferris wheel!" In my rearview mirror, I could see fear growing in her eyes. "No, Daddy", she said, "I can't. I don't want to." I said, "Kharis, you know, you're just going to have to be brave. Sometimes you just have to try new things." It was not like I was asking her to go through that creepy clown exhibit or anything. She looked down and said, "I know, Daddy . . . sometimes I feel like I'm just a big scaredy-cat."

Honestly I was a little frustrated at this point, and I said triumphantly, "That's right, Kharis. Sometimes you are a scaredy-cat, and you'll never go anywhere in life until you become brave." My four-year-old, Allie, who was listening to all of this, looked over at her with the sweetest, most sincere expression and said, "No, Kharis, you are NOT a scaredy-cat. You are my big sister."

I felt like someone had slapped me in the face with a two by four. I thought, *Great. My four-year-old is the voice of the Holy Spirit, and I am the voice of Satan.*

Satan has tricked so many of us into believing his voice is actually the voice of the Holy Spirit. We've grown so accustomed to the voice of condemnation that we think the only thing the Holy Spirit ever says to us is, "Stop it! Stop it! Stop it! What's wrong with you? You're terrible!" He speaks altogether different: "I have made you, My child. I have taken away all your sin. I could not approve of you more than I do right now. Live that way."[3]

Think of what Jesus said to the woman caught in the act of adultery, He said to her, "Neither do I condemn you; go and sin no more" (John 8:11 NKJV). What is most significant about His statement is its order: promise first; command second. "Neither do I condemn you" precedes "go and sin no more." We almost always try to reverse those. We say, "If you can manage to go and sin no more, then God will accept you."

God, however, motivates us *from* acceptance, not toward it. Jesus' affirmation would give this woman the security that could free her from her destructive relationship with sex. Without that, she'd never truly break free. God's approval is the power that liberates us from sin, not the reward for having liberated ourselves.

Embracing Your New Identity

Many people can't shake some failure that stains their past. Perhaps there is a voice inside that whispers to your soul, "See? That proves it. Look at what you did. You are a failure. You are no good."

That is the voice of your enemy. What must you do? Embrace your identity in the gospel. In Christ, God couldn't love you any more than He does right now.

Maybe you're not as successful as you always thought you'd be. Maybe you feel like you let your parents, your family, or yourself down. Maybe you sense a general spirit of disapproval over your life—from coworkers, your friends, your spouse, your parents, and from God. In a thousand different ways they tell you, "You're not good enough. You're a disappointment."

Preach the gospel to yourself. You must tell yourself that because of Jesus you have the absolute approval of the only One whose opinion really matters.

Maybe you have the opposite problem—maybe you've always been "a winner." You've always compared favorably to everyone else and so your self-esteem is high. I've seen that carry a lot of people far in life—until they finally meet someone better than them. Or they face a failure. If you find your identity in your success, you're going to go through cycles of pride and despair. You're proud and domineering when you are on top, and you annoy everyone. Yet, you also live in a constant state of paranoia, always worried about someone taking away your success. If this is you, preach the gospel to yourself. Remind yourself that God's acceptance is all that matters and that it lasts forever. It has been given to you as a gift; earned by Christ, not by you. There's no room for pride.

Maybe you are disturbed at how few of the fruits of the Spirit are present in your life. Do you ever think, *How could anyone who is truly saved be as messed up as I am?* I think that sometimes. When I look into my heart I still see a frustratingly small amount of generosity displaced by an overwhelming amount of selfishness. Jealously and pride still pop up like

> *My identity and my security are in God's acceptance of me given as a gift in Christ.*

weeds. When I start to base my spiritual identity on how much progress I have made, I start to despair.

My identity and my security are not in my spiritual progress. My identity and my security are in God's acceptance of me given as a gift in Christ. And that's good, because if anything, I am more, not less, aware of my sin than I was ten years ago.

Get this: That is spiritual progress. To grow in awareness of the depths of sin God has saved you from *is* growth in the gospel.

Do you worry a lot? Worry springs from not being convinced of a sovereign God's absolute love for you. Worry disappears when you realize that God loves you unfailingly and will let nothing interrupt His plans for your good.

You see, to all of these emotions—fear, insecurity, false-confidence, despair, worry—we must preach the gospel. We must tell ourselves, daily, that there is nothing we could do that would make God love us more and nothing we have done makes Him love us less, and His love is perfectly in control of our lives.

> To all of these emotions—fear, insecurity, false-confidence, despair, worry—we must preach the gospel.

Our sin and our failures have not, and can never again, separate us from Him. He has put them away forever, as far, as the east is from the west (Ps. 103:12). We have been credited, once and for all, the righteousness of Jesus Christ. He has said to us in Christ, "You are My beloved child. In you I am well pleased . . . I will never leave you or forsake you," and "surely goodness and mercy will follow you all the days of your life. You will dwell in My house forever" (Matt. 17:5; Heb. 13:5; Ps. 23:6, author paraphrase).

Abide in Jesus

Have you felt those words in the depth of your heart? Abiding in Jesus means reminding ourselves constantly that there is nothing we could ever do that would make God love us more, and nothing we have done that makes Him love us less.

- What about if you gave away all your money, wouldn't He love you just a little bit more? *Nope.*
- What if you went to live on the foreign mission field? *No again.*
- What if you finally began to treat your spouse with grace? *Nada.*
- What if you took out the trash for her like she asked? *She might love you more, but God wouldn't.*
- What if you went one full-week without a single, lustful thought? *God's acceptance of you is based on the fact that Christ went a lifetime without sinning against Him in even the slightest way. Now, you are in Him and He is in you. Thus, God could not love you more than He does right now, because He loves Christ perfectly.*

You must dwell on this great truth *daily.* Sometimes hourly. Sometimes every minute. It is the only way to drive out fear, unbelief, and temptation.

> *You must dwell on God's great truth daily. It is the only way to drive out fear, unbelief, and temptation.*

Why so often? Because, again, you are hardwired for works-righteousness. When you're not deliberately thinking gospel, you've probably slipped back into self-justification mode. It's a lot like the plastic rodents in that "whack-a-mole" game you play at the fair. Just when you've knocked one down, another appears from a different place. The moment we take our eyes off of the gospel, those rodents of self-righteousness and self-condemnation spring back up. So, we must pound them with the counterintuitive truth of the gospel: God's acceptance is given to us, in its entirety, as a gift we receive by faith, to the praise and glory of God.

> *The moment we take our eyes off of the gospel, those rodents of self-righteousness and self-condemnation spring back up.*

Make your home in that awareness. As you do, you will abound in fruitfulness.

So I'd encourage you to pray some form of this prayer daily, starting right now:

"In Christ, there is nothing I can do that would make You love me more, and nothing I have done that makes You love me less."

CHAPTER 4

Changed without a Command

"In Christ, there is nothing I can do
that would make You love me more, and nothing
I have done that makes You love me less."

Hopefully you're beginning to see that dwelling on that simple truth of the gospel leads to organic, natural outgrowth. Perhaps you've already experienced how doing so has changed your life.

The Bible gives us several case studies in how this works. One of my favorites is the story of Zacchaeus. Zacchaeus went from being one of the most selfish men in ancient Israel to the most generous—instantaneously, without being commanded to.

Meet Zacchaeus

Zacchaeus was not a good man. In fact, he was a downright bad man. A wee, little, bad man.

The Romans had problems collecting taxes from conquered cities. The people would buy and trade on the black market and evade the tax. A transplanted Roman official would not be familiar enough with the city's underside to know where all the real money was.

So the Romans hired a native from the conquered city to collect the tax for them—someone who would know where the money was hiding. The tax collectors were then given a garrison of soldiers to assist them. The Romans did not care how much extra the tax collectors collected for themselves. As long as they got their share, they turned their heads. As you can imagine, tax collectors got very, very rich.

In other words, Zacchaeus' substantial wealth came from selling out his family and friends to an imperial foreign power. Zacchaeus evidently didn't care, however. He loved money. That's the only way you would ever consent to being a tax collector. Money had to be worth more to you than everything.

Seriously—can you imagine a worse person?

The Jewish *Mishnah* said that tax collectors were so loathsome that they should not even be considered people. You were free to lie to tax collectors, it said, because lying to an animal was not a sin. You can catch a glimpse of how unpopular Zacchaeus was in the fact that he had to climb a tree to see Jesus. (If a short person wants to stand in front of you in a crowd, you usually just let them, because they don't really affect your line of sight. But no one moved for Zacchaeus. They hip-checked him right in the face every time he made a move forward. Hence the tree-climbing.)

Zacchaeus Meets Jesus

But then the unexpected happened. Jesus looked up into Zacchaeus's tree and said, "Zacchaeus, come down. I'm coming to your house for dinner."

What exactly was said *at* that dinner party we don't know, but we do know the effect it had on the Zacchaeus. He said, "I will pay back anything I've stolen four times." On top of that, he gave away 50 percent of his treasures to the poor.

There is no record of Jesus' commanding Zacchaeus to respond like that. In fact, Zacchaeus goes way beyond the Levitical requirements of restitution. There was only one time that you have to pay back four times, and that was if you'd stolen somebody's cow. (Don't know why that is? Maybe you caused them *udder* financial ruin or something.) And there is certainly nothing in the law about giving away 50 percent. Zacchaeus evidently just did it because he felt like it.

New Testament scholars say there is a certain playfulness in the way Zacchaeus informs Jesus of what he's about to do. He's not like, "Oh Sovereign Lord, in humble response to Your requirement, I give what Thou demands. Please accept my humble offerings in due recompense for the wicked things I have done." The tone of Zack's language is, instead, rather kid-like. Almost, "Look, Dad, watch . . . look at what I'm doing! Look, Dad, no hands!"

He's bubbling over with giddy generosity. He's tipsy on giving. He's not giving away money because he has to—he's giving away money because *he wants to.*

What Caused the Change?

Zacchaeus went from being a man who sold his soul to the god of money to a man who got a buzz from giving it away. What caused that change? The focus of the story is on how Jesus treated Zacchaeus, the sinner. Jesus called Zacchaeus down from the tree when everyone else shut him out.

We also know that Jesus went to eat with Zacchaeus before he repented. In that day, to share a meal with someone was a sign of acceptance, even of intimate fellowship. To eat with someone meant that you were embracing them.

The Jewish leaders understandably objected: "What is He doing eating with a guy who is a known sinner? How can He communicate love and acceptance to that guy?"

But Jesus produced in Zacchaeus, in that moment, something the Jewish law had not been able to. Jesus looked at a wee little bad man in a tree—who was there because he was despised, an outcast, and rightfully so—and gave him an invitation of acceptance and intimacy.

That experience changed Zacchaeus forever. Every other religion in the world would have said to Zacchaeus, "If you change, you can find God. If you change, you can find acceptance and salvation."

But the gospel is the opposite of religion. Jesus said to Zacchaeus, "Zacchaeus, salvation has *come to you*. You didn't go out and find salvation. It has found you."

> Zacchaeus was not changed by a command of Jesus, but by an experience with Jesus.

Zacchaeus was not changed by a command of Jesus, but by an experience with Jesus.

When Zacchaeus tasted of God's grace, he was transformed from a man of greedy exploitation to one of lavish,
exuberant, bubbly generosity.

The law produces Pharisees; the gospel produces Christians

Unfortunately most preachers still think that preaching
the law in some way is how we can change our congregations.
"Do tithe." "Do give sacrificially." "Do downsize." Around our
church we call those "do-do" sermons. They give you a list of
things to do and make you feel worthless when you don't do
them. Preaching of this type might sometimes produce a large
offering, but they produce nothing of real value in God's sight.

The preaching of the law produces only Pharisees.[1] They
might be Pharisees who fast twice a week, tithe their spices
and cumin, and refuse to walk more than a certain amount of
steps on the Sabbath. Or, they might be Pharisees who give
away lots of money, adopt children, and go on mission trips.
Either way, they are only Pharisees. Their focus is on external
change, while their hearts are filled with poison. They are
immaculately obedient tombs.

Give the Pharisees their due credit: they were quite zealous in their obedience. Many gave away lots of money. Some
travelled the world in search of converts (see Matt. 23:15).
They were always at prayer meetings and no doubt the first
ones to sign up for volunteer teams. But they were also bitter,
resentful, dissatisfied, and self-focused. And they hated Jesus
Christ.

God does not want Pharisees. He wants people who overflow with the joy of serving Jesus.

Transformed not by a command of Jesus, but by an experience with Jesus

Like Zacchaeus, we will not be transformed by the command *of* Jesus; we will be transformed by an experience *with* Jesus. As I'll explain in part 3, obedience to commands is an essential part of the Christian life, but the power for transformation doesn't come from them. The power for transformation comes from the gospel. We are changed not by being told what we need to do for God, but by hearing the news about what God has done for us.

> We are changed not by being told what we need to do for God, but by hearing the news about what God has done for us.

Thus, rather than enumerating a list of commands to obey, true gospel preaching highlights a story—a story about God that reveals such power and beauty that you are never the same once you have encountered it.

If you've ever watched one of those "epic movies," the plot is always basically the same:[2] (Take, for example, the 2010 blockbuster *Avatar.*) You have some loser guy with no purpose in life, no direction, no courage . . . but then he's swept up into some great, thrilling drama, in which he experiences real danger and encounters real beauty and is fundamentally changed by the experience. (In the case of *Avatar*, more like a creepy beauty with a blue tail. Like a tall version of the Smurfs.) He returns to the real world a completely different person. He is no longer afraid of normal dangers. Why? He's seen real danger and overcome it. He is no longer dominated by normal, everyday temptations. Why? Because he's tasted real beauty.

That's what happens when you meet God in the story of Jesus. You get swept up into a story of such cosmic drama and beauty that you are forever changed. Your behavior is radically altered because you've seen and tasted something from a completely different world.

Gospel change is the Spirit of God using the story of God to make the beauty of God come alive in our hearts. Having our eyes opened to see our part in that story creates in us a love for God that is strong enough to finally drive out our attraction to other idols. The gospel cures us of fear, dissatisfaction, and pride.

> Gospel change is the Spirit of God using the story of God to make the beauty of God come alive in our hearts.

Paul describes this Zacchaeus-style process of change to his young pastor-friend, Titus:

For the grace of God has appeared, bringing salvation for all people, training us to renounce ungodliness and worldly passions and to live self-controlled, upright, and godly lives in the present age, waiting for our blessed hope, the appearing of the glory of our great God and Savior Jesus Christ, who gave himself for us to redeem us from all lawlessness and to purify for himself a people . . . who are zealous for good works. (Titus 2:11–14)

That's a pretty exhaustive list of righteous living, isn't it? "Renouncing ungodliness and worldly passions"; "living self-controlled, upright and godly lives"; "waiting" eagerly for Jesus to return . . . But *how* does Paul say we develop these things? What is it that *trains* us to do them? Bible memorization? Accountability partners? Being baptized in the Spirit? Radical devotion?

Not that they don't have their place, but Paul points to none of those here: It is *"the grace of God,"* Paul says, that trains us to *"renounce ungodliness and worldly passions and to live self-controlled, upright, and godly lives."* Think about, Paul says, how the grace of God came into the world for you, pursuing you to the cross. The God of the universe *"gave himself for us,"* made us His own, and will *appear* again to take you home with all the glory and splendor and power that brought Him out of the grave.

When we get swept up into that story of grace, we will be "zealous for good works." We will even long for His appearing. Very few people in other religions long to stand before God. Most are absolutely terrified by that. I lived in a Muslim context for a while and know that while Muslims are fervently committed to Allah, most do not "long" to see Him. The idea of standing before Allah is terrifying.

The gospel of God's mercy, however, creates longing for God. Because we know we are safe before Him, and we know the love He showed to us in the gospel, we long to see Him.

So Paul tells Titus to preach to his people the great story of grace, because only then they will live rightly. He doesn't tell them "try harder" or "learn more." His focus is not on behaving; it's on *believing*.

Threats, commands, and action steps will only change our behavior externally. Getting caught up into the story of Jesus changes our hearts.

Preaching the beauty and unfathomable grace of Jesus

So how then do we compel true, heart-centered change, both in ourselves and others? We tell the story of grace.

We help them see what Zacchaeus saw. We actually have an advantage on the diminutive tree-climbing tax collector, because we are able, on this side of the cross, to see the grace of Jesus even more clearly than he could.

Why was Zacchaeus in the tree? Because he was despised. Jesus would end His ministry hung on a tree in derision. Jesus called Zacchaeus down from the place of shame and into the place of honor, and took Zacchaeus's place on the tree.

The grace of God extended to us at the cross should blow our minds. We "stand amazed in the presence of Jesus the Nazarene, and wonder how He could love me, a sinner condemned unclean."

There is no way to understand what Jesus did for you, on a heart level, and not be radically changed. Grace changes wee-little-stingy sinners into saints of magnificent generosity.

I hope you will worship as you pray:

⚬⚬⚬

"In Christ, there is nothing I can do that would make You love me more, and nothing I have done that makes You love me less."

CHAPTER 5

God Is Better

What do you really feel like has to be present in your life for you to be happy? For life to be worth living?

Maybe, if you were really honest, you'd have to admit that it's money. Or the acclaim of others. Or power. Or family. Friends, even church.

Is it God? Is He what you most desire and want? Is His presence the one, indispensable thing you could not live without?

The first part of The Gospel Prayer reflects on our assurance of God's acceptance of us in Christ. The second part of the prayer moves us to reflect on how great a treasure that acceptance is. How important is God's approval in your life? It's one thing to know that God has accepted you fully in Christ; it's another thing for that to become the weightiest and most defining reality in your life.

The second part of the prayer goes like this:

> *"Your presence and approval are all*
> *I need for everlasting joy."*

This second part of The Gospel Prayer deals with our propensity toward idolatry.

Idol Factories

An idol is whatever takes the place of God in our lives. An idol is whatever we feel like we could not live without; it is what we think is an absolute necessity for life and happiness.

Idols are the things that we give the most "weight" to. They become so heavy that we can't imagine our lives without them. An idol is not necessarily a bad thing. It's usually a good thing that we've made into a god-thing that then becomes a bad thing to us.[1]

In Exodus 20:1–5, God says that an idol is something that (a) we "bow down to," which means it commands our obedience. It is something that (b) we "serve," which means we pursue it because we feel like we couldn't live without it. As such, it controls our emotions. We are terrified at the prospect of not obtaining it. Finally, it is something we (c) love more than God. God is jealous for our love, and if possessing something brings us more joy than God does, it has become an idol. Tim Keller has said that an idol is behind our loftiest dreams, our scariest nightmares, and our most unyielding emotions.[2]

John Calvin said that the human heart is an "idol factory," constantly latching god-like weight onto created things.

Idolatry was behind the first sin, and it has been behind every sin since then.

So what is that for you? What have you given god-like weight in your life? I'm going to ask you some questions—if you answer these questions honestly, you'll probably start to see some recurring themes. These are most likely what you have substituted for God.

> John Calvin said that the human heart is an "idol factory."

The "Idolatry-Detector" Test

What one thing do you most hope is in your future? Career success? A certain salary? Owning your own home? Owning a second one at the beach? Getting married? Seeing your kids grow up to be successful? Having the respect of your teammates? Going pro? Being loved and respected by your colleagues?

What is it that, without it, life would hardly seem worth living?

What is the one thing you most worry about losing? What one thing could you just absolutely not get along without? Your family? Your job? The love of your spouse? The respect of your kids?

I used to obsess about my retirement investments because I was afraid I'd make some financial mistake, lose it all, and have to work an hourly wage greeting people at the front entrance of Walmart. Money in the bank is a security I often feel like I need for the good life, so I often worry about losing it.

Sometimes I fear losing my influence in my church. I fear that as I get older I'll lose my edge and people will quit coming to hear me preach. I have this recurring nightmare where I show up one Sunday morning and everyone has gone to a new church where a hotter new preacher is lighting it up. I show up in our big auditorium and it's just me and my wife, and she is sitting on the front row listening to a sermon by Matt Chandler on her iPod.

I'm not saying we should be excited, or even apathetic, about losing any of those things. The question is whether or not they are so valuable to us that their loss would be unsustainable.

If you could change one thing about yourself right now, what would it be? Would you lose thirty pounds? Would you change your looks? Your marital status? Your job? Your zip code? Would you have your kids come home?

Whatever you come up with, you probably want to change that thing because you think that if you did you'd be so much happier. There is certainly nothing wrong with desiring to change our lives. But when we couldn't imagine being happy unless something changes, we have an idol.

What thing have you sacrificed most for? Sacrifice and worship almost always go hand in hand. What have you worked the hardest for? To get the scholarship? To obtain the perfect body? To land the job? To be the best in your field? To get to a certain income level?

What you prize most is shown by what you pursue the hardest.

Who is there in your life that you feel like you can't forgive, and why? An ex-husband ruined your reputation and stole the best years of your life? Your wife who cheated on you and publicly humiliated you? An irresponsible or unethical partner who ruined your business? A close friend who stole your boyfriend? A drunk driver who killed your child?

Many times our inability to forgive is connected to the fact that someone took away from us something we feel like we can't be happy without. There is nothing wrong with regretting, deeply, the loss of any of those things. When you cannot forgive someone, however, it is usually because they took something from you that you depended on for life, happiness, and security. They stole something from you that you think can never be replaced, and you cannot stop hating them for it.

What has left you bitter? What has happened in your past that you just can't shake? Were you overlooked for a promotion, or cheated out of an opportunity? Was it being abused by a parent, or being betrayed by a spouse or friend?

Bitterness is almost always tied to idolatry. Someone took something from you that you thought was necessary for life.

When do you feel the most significant? When do you hold your head up the highest? What is there that you hope people find out about you? Do you constantly mention your job, or the job you think you're going to have when you graduate, or where you got your degree from? Are you always looking for ways to show off your house or car? Does your heart soar with pride when you talk about your kids? If you're a pastor, do you love it when people ask you how big your church is? Or do you hate that because it's small? Do you love it when people compare you positively to other pastors?

Your identity is whatever makes you feel the most signifi-cant. What makes you feel the most significant is what you put the most weight upon.

What triggers depression in you? That your kids never call? The fact that your marriage doesn't look like it's ever going to get better? Is it that you have reached a certain age and still aren't married? Is it when you don't get the recognition you know you deserve?[3] Is it how little you've accomplished? Is it that no matter how hard you try, your church still won't grow?

Depression is triggered when something we deemed essential for life and happiness is denied to us.

(Please note: I'm not trying to gloss over some of the physiological factors in depression. Often there are some. I am simply saying that sometimes our depression is *fueled* by our idolatry.)

Where do you turn for comfort when things are not going well? Maybe you bury yourself in your work to numb the fact that your wife ignores you and your kids are drifting away from you. Or perhaps you find escape in the arms of a lover.

Some sensual pleasure, like pornography or comfort food? Perhaps alcohol or a drug?

Maybe you turn inward to some truth about yourself that comforts you. I've often comforted myself in disappointment by reminding myself of some talent I had. In high school, when I was depressed because my athletic career was not tak-ing off, I told myself my academic ability set me apart.

My wife struggled with a mild eating disorder in col-lege. She felt like she needed to have a great body to have any real worth. But she also found comfort in food. She'd get depressed because she didn't see how she could be happy if she didn't lose weight. Her depression drove her to comfort food. It was a vicious cycle created by the fact that two of her gods were in conflict with one another.

> St. Augustine said that things like worry, fear, sadness, and deep depression are "smoke from the fires" rising from the altars of our idolatry.

Do those questions reveal certain patterns in your life? St. Augustine said that things like worry, fear, sadness, and deep depression are "smoke from the fires" rising from the altars of our idolatry. Follow the trail of that smoke and you'll see where you have substituted something for God.

Trying to make God an accomplice in our idolatry

Astoundingly we often try to make God an accomplice in the pursuit of our idols. James, the half brother of Jesus, said that sometimes when we pray, we don't get what we ask for because, "you ask wrongly, to spend it on your passions. You adulterous people! Do you not know that friendship with the world is enmity with God?" (James 4:3–4).

We can "pray like adulterers." That's a pretty disturbing analogy, but what does it mean? An adulterer is someone who finds in another the intimacy they should be finding in their spouse. We are adulterers to God when we demand that He give us certain things so that we can find a happiness, contentment, and security in these things that really we should be finding in Him.

- "God, I just *have to be* married or I'll be miserable! "
- "God, we *just have to* have children."

- "God, why *haven't You* healed me? It's not fair."
- "God, I *have to* get into medical school."

Asking for any of the above things is not wrong, but when our joy *depends* on obtaining those things, we have become spiritual adulterers. We have given a weightiness that we should be giving to God to something else. And we're asking God to help us in the process of obtaining those things.

> We are adulterers to God when we demand that He give us certain things so that we can find a happiness, contentment, and security that really we should be finding in Him.

Imagine if I said to my wife, "Sweetheart, you remember that on July 28, 2000, you vowed to meet my romantic and sexual needs?" "Yes." I continue, "Well, I have decided that what I need to be fulfilled romantically and sexually is to have an affair. Can you arrange that for me?" How is my wife likely to react to that proposition?

If you don't know her, be assured that's probably the last conversation I'd ever have, period. When we got married, she vowed to satisfy these desires in herself. She didn't sign up to become my pimp.

Needless to say, God will not be anybody's pimp.

Our idols leave us empty

Ultimately idols leave us empty because our hearts were created for God. To use the words of the seventeenth-century philosopher Blaise Pascal, God created our hearts with a vacuum. We search for something to fulfill our deepest cravings, but nothing on earth works because the vacuum was created by the absence of God. Anything we substitute for God in that place leaves us still yearning. Or, as St. Augustine put it, *"You have made us for Yourself, Lord. Our hearts are restless, until they find their rest in You."*

Your heart was created in such a way that only the eternal love of God can satisfy it. A marriage partner, no matter how perfect for you, cannot play the role of God in your life. Remember that scene in *Jerry Maguire* where Tom Cruise says to Renee Zelwegger, "You complete me." Most of us dream about finding someone who completes us; who makes all our unhappiness, insecurity, and meaninglessness go away.

After watching a number of marriages come together and break apart over the years, I can confidently say that insecure, lonely single people become insecure, lonely married people. Problems like loneliness and insecurity are not cured by another human being; they are only cured by God. Your soul was created first and foremost for God, not for romance. Your marriage partner, no matter how perfectly suited for you, can never play the role of God in your life.

> *Problems like loneliness and insecurity are not cured by another human being; they are only cured by God.*

What happens in most marriages is that you have a girl floating in a sea of loneliness and despair, when along comes a 6'5" studly, well-built life preserver. And, of course, she does what any drowning person would do—she clings to him for dear life. And she suffocates the life out of him, because he, try as he may, can't meet those needs in her life. He wasn't designed to. Only God can.

We weren't created for another human being, we were created for God.

Money—another idol of choice—can't satisfy us, either. Like marriage, money can be a great blessing from God. But money cannot provide lasting security or genuine fulfillment. Just look at the people who have money—do they look secure, happy, and fulfilled? Years ago I heard of a Fortune 500 CEO who said, "I spent all my life climbing the ladder of success, only to find out it was leaning against the wrong building."

Whatever idol you choose, the result will still be the same. Idols promise fulfillment but deliver disillusionment. And that's just the beginning.

Idolatry also produces anxiety and fear in our hearts. We live afraid, knowing that if our idol is taken from us, life will be miserable. The economy might crash again, wiping out what little is left in our retirement. We might never get married. Our business might fail. A loved one might get cancer.

First John 4:18 says that only "perfect love" casts out fear. Idols can't love perfectly, but God can. God's love is perfect in (a) its intensity toward us (God could not love us more than He already does); (b) its ability to satisfy us (we are created to be satisfied fully by the love of God); and (c) its control of all things in our lives (we know that the God who controls all the universe loves us and will never leave us and is control-ling every molecule in the universe to work out His good and perfect plan for our lives). Resting in His perfect love drives out any fear and worry. No idol can ever give you that, because no other idol is that loving, that fulfilling, or that powerful.

Jesus Satisfies

Jesus is the one essential thing that we must have. He is life itself.

Jesus is better than money. God owns all the money and He's our Father; He promises to give us whatever we need. And God never crashes or dips below 10,000.

Jesus is better than human love. You and I have never experienced tenderness and affection like God showed to us when He took us in His arms at the cross.

Jesus is better than any earthly pleasure. God is the fountain of all pleasure. Earthly pleasures, C. S. Lewis famously said, are supposed to function like rays of the sun that direct us back to their source.[4] As the ray warms our face, we look back up along the ray to its source. Marriage, sex, money, children, friends, good food are all shadows and reflections of true goodness. For a while, some "cloud" may obstruct a ray from hitting our face. We might remain single when we'd like to be married. We might be poor when we'd like to be rich. Death may take one of our children. The rays of the sun will at times be shielded from our eyes, but the sun itself remains.

After the first date I went on with my wife, a friend asked me the next day what I thought about her. I ripped out a piece of notebook paper and scribbled down some 60+ adjectives that described her. I put down one-word descriptions of her personality, her smile, her mind, even her toes.

I showed it to him and said, "That's what I thought about her. I'm going to marry her." After we got engaged, I went back and found that piece of paper and had it framed. On our wedding day I gave it to her with the caption under it, "You represent something that can never be taken away from me." I know she, herself, could be taken away. But she

> Jesus is the one essential thing that we must have. He is life itself.

represents something that can *never* be taken away from me, and that is the beauty and love of the Father God. As Jonathan Edwards said, "Pleasure is the ray, God's love is the sun. Pleasure is the shadow; God's love is the substance. Pleasure is the stream, God's love is the ocean."[5]

Jesus is better than earthly power. There is no greater sense of empowerment than to know that the sovereign God who directs every molecule in the universe is working in all things for our good. *That* is real power.

Jesus is better than popularity. What good is earthly fame if you are famous only to a bunch of nobodies? To be known and honored by the God of the universe, that is better than the approbations of millions of little no-account earthlings.

John Piper, after giving a list similar to the one I gave above, says, "And on and on it goes . . . everything the world has to offer, God is better and more abiding. There is no comparison. God wins, every time."[6]

Our ability to be joyful in all things is the measure of how much we believe the gospel

Sometimes we know that Christ has taken all of our sin, but His approval just doesn't carry that much weight in our lives. Other things matter more to us.

The amount which you understand the gospel is measured by your ability to be joyful in all circumstances. If you grasp what a treasure the presence and acceptance of God are, then even when life goes really wrong you will have a joy that sustains you, because you'll recognize the value of what you have in Him. When life punches you in the face, you'll say, "But I still have the love and acceptance of God, a treasure I don't deserve." And the joy you find in that treasure can make you rejoice even when you have a bloody nose. You have a joy that death or deprivation cannot touch. This is why Paul could say from the confines of a Roman prison: "Rejoice in the Lord *always*; again I will say, Rejoice" (Phil. 4:4, author emphasis).

If the Coach Is Happy, I Am Happy

When I was in college, I coached a twelve-year-old boys' soccer team. We were pretty good, and we had gone through the season undefeated. My band of twelve-year-old studs strutted into the playoff season with undaunted confidence. The first playoff game was held at night, and no one on the team, including me, thought defeat was possible.

Well, we got crushed. The final score didn't really reflect it—we only lost 3 to 1. But the other team absolutely dominated the field of play. And the worst of it was that their star player was . . . ahemm . . . a girl. She was the greatest twelve-year-old player I had ever seen. She dominated. She took shot after shot on goal, and I was sick of it.

So, with about ten minutes left to go in the second half, down 2 to 1, I pulled out one of our best defensive players and told him, "David, I am sick and tired of that girl getting all those shots on goal."

"Me too, Coach."

"David, you have one assignment for the rest of the game, and it is that girl. Whenever she comes within fifteen yards of our penalty box with the ball, I want her on her rear end. You understand that?"

"Yes sir, Coach."

"I mean it, David. She is your whole responsibility. You understand me? David, I don't care if the guy next to you bursts into flames. That is not your responsibility. She is."

"I got it, Coach."

As David turned around to go back on the field, I said, "David, do it *legally*."

We had worked on this in practice. The glorious slide-tackle. It was now our only hope.

With just five minutes left to go in the game, female Maradona got the ball about midfield and began to make her way down the right side. She went through the left fullback like he was invisible. She cut her way back to the center, and she did something there to the stopper—I'm not sure what—but the next thing I knew he was in the fetal position crying for his momma. Now, just her, the sweeper, and the goalie. She pump-faked with her right leg and both the sweeper and goalie fell on the ground. Either that or they just evaporated—

I'm still not sure which. But now it was just her and a wide-open goal.

And, then, behold. He came.

Out of the left side of my peripheral vision an orange blur appeared. Moving silently, stealthily, but at full-speed. *David*, the obedient twelve-year-old defender. Tractor beam locked on her, bearing down with deadly precision, he hit her, from behind, in the full spread-eagle attack position.

There was a thud, a cloud of dust, and then silence. Eerie silence. Somewhere in the distance a vulture crooned. (I might be adding a few details to this story for some dramatic flair, but you get the drift.)

It was one of those moments when everyone was like, *"Did that just happen?"* And then, all at once, almost as if a movie director had suddenly yelled "action," everyone erupted into anger. Their team was angry because they thought we tried to take out their star player. The referee was angry, trying to figure out if it was appropriate to give a twelve-year-old a red card and throw him out for the season. Our team was angry because they realized David had just handed them a penalty kick in the penalty box, which they were sure to score on. The soccer moms were angry because they thought "psycho-coach" sent in this poor little kid to go "angry-birds" on an innocent girl.

David slowly stood up, and, like a perfect little gentleman, helped the girl up. Then, to my horror, turned to me and gave me a grin and a big thumbs-up, removing all doubt from the parents as to who was behind this attack. (All I could hear in my mind was the term *lawsuit*.)

I pulled David out of the game and said, "David—what were you thinking? What's wrong with you, son?"

David looked up at me with a perfectly innocent twelve-year-old face, and said, "Coach . . . but you told me to take her out . . . *illegally*."

David thought the last thing I told him as he went into the game was to take this girl out *il*-legally. "Take her out, David . . . and David—make it nasty."

There is at least one thing that is very impressive—touching, even—about David's obedience. David knew there could be severe consequences for his action. He knew it would cost us a penalty kick. He knew he'd probably get a red card. He knew he'd probably get grounded by his parents . . . and maybe even jumped on the playground after the game.

But he didn't care, really, about any of those things. What did he care about? My approval. In his little (warped?), twelve-year-old mind, he thought, "Coach is my hero. It doesn't matter what else happens. If *the coach* is happy, I am happy." He was willing to face whatever consequences if I was pleased with him.

Jesus is to carry that kind of weight in our lives. Obedience to Him is costly, but His presence and approval are worth anything we forsake or any consequence we incur. He really is that glorious. He is the treasure worth forsaking all else to obtain.

Freed to Enjoy the Rest

Learning to be satisfied in Jesus will free you to enjoy everything else. Being fulfilled in Christ means that you no longer depend on other things for life and happiness. That means you can enjoy them, because you are no longer enslaved by them. The prospect of losing them doesn't terrorize you. And you can say "no" to them when they are not God's will.

The great irony is that you can really only begin to enjoy money, romance, and sex when you don't depend on them for life. C. S. Lewis said it like this: In life, there are first things (God) and second things (everything else). If you put first things first, you'll also get the second things. If you put second things first, you'll not only lose the first things but you'll lose the second things too.[7] When Jesus is your life, you can start to enjoy the rest of your life.

When you are satisfied with God's presence and approval in your life, you will no longer obsess about what everyone else thinks about you. You can quit hiding your faults and start living with authenticity, letting people see the real you—the "you" with all the faults and warts—because you no longer depend on their admiration for personal fulfillment.

It is a revolutionary, liberating truth: in Christ, you have all you need for everlasting joy. His approval and presence are all that you need for life and happiness.

He is the *only* One who should play the role of God in our lives. He has no equals, no partners, and doesn't want to share the office of "God" with anyone.

If you're like me, you probably need to remind yourself of that every day:

⟨⟨⟨⟩⟩⟩

"Your presence and approval are all
I need for everlasting joy."

CHAPTER 6

Changed by Sight

Sight is one of those things I took for granted until I was confronted with the possibility of losing it.

Shortly after I got married I heard an ad on the radio by a doctor offering laser eye surgery for a ridiculously low price. It didn't occur to me that contracting out your eyeballs to the lowest bidder was not really a good idea.

I think it was the fastening of the strap around my head that finally triggered in my mind what was about to happen. Suddenly it became crystal clear that they were about to remove my cornea and reform my retina with a high-powered incineration laser.

Now helpless, I watched the little knife slice off the cornea of my right eye (I realize that doesn't sound like the kind of thing you *want* to watch . . . but where else is there to look at that moment?) After the cornea was removed, I was treated to a two-minute kaleidoscopic light show, coupled with a curious burning-rubber smell . . . and though two minutes doesn't sound like a long time, it feels like days when your cornea is in a petri dish on the table beside you.

All I could think about the whole time was, "What if there is an earthquake?" Earthquakes are not common where I live in North Carolina, but I've watched the History Channel's *Unexpected Mega Disasters* enough to know that there's no telling when the next big one is coming.

Thankfully, no earthquake. And the whole process, for both eyes, lasted only about fifteen minutes. The doctor replaced the cornea on my eye, painted it over with a little eyeball-super-glue, sat me up, and ever since then I've been able to see 20/20.

For those of you considering laser eye surgery, be encouraged.

I realize I probably wasn't in any real danger of never seeing again. But lying there during the surgery I had some sober moments to reflect on the value of my sight. Without sight there is so much of life that we'd miss. We wouldn't know the beauties of color or the majesty of a sunset. We wouldn't know the thrill that comes into our hearts from seeing a look of delight on our children's faces or the affectionate gaze of our spouse.

Spiritual sight is even more important. Spiritual sight is how we perceive God. Without spiritual sight you miss out on the most glorious display in the universe. And the tragedy is that if you are spiritually blind you have no idea that you're missing anything at all.

Once we have our eyes opened to the beauty of God, we can really start to understand the second part of The Gospel Prayer:

"Your presence and approval are all
I need for everlasting joy."

The apostle Paul says spiritual sight is what changes us. Seeing the love of God and the glory of Christ is what restructures our hearts and reorders our desires (2 Cor. 3:18; 4:4).

That's why twice in the book of Ephesians Paul asks God to give the Ephesians spiritual sight. He says, "I pray . . .

. . . that the God of our Lord Jesus Christ, the Father of glory, may give you a spirit of wisdom and of revelation in the knowledge of him, having the eyes of your hearts enlightened, that you may know what is the hope . . . and his power . . . (Eph. 1:17–19)

and that

[you] may have strength to comprehend . . . the love of Christ." (Eph. 3:18–19)

Paul's second prayer comes right in the middle of the book of Ephesians. The first three chapters were deep gospel doctrine; the last three are remarkably relevant instruction for living. Christian teachers often debate which is the more important of those two: the doctrine or the application. I suspect Paul would say that while both are important, the

> *Doctrine helps describe the God we must see; application helps us see how to love the God we have seen.*

most important thing of all is seeing the beauty and glory of God revealed in the gospel. When the glory of God is seen in the gospel, changes occur naturally. The goal of preaching, then, is neither the conveyance of information nor instruction in application. The goal of preaching is worship.

Doctrine helps describe the God we must see; application helps us see how to love the God we have seen. But both are useless if the eyes of the heart have not been opened to see and savor the beauty of God.

Seeing What Israel Saw

Just as Paul prayed for the Ephesians, the first thing God did when He led the children of Israel out of slavery in Egypt was open their eyes to who He is. Exodus 19 says that He descended upon Mount Sinai, wrapping it in smoke and thick darkness. Lightning and thunder filled the skies. A sound like a trumpet pierced the air, growing louder and louder until it was almost unbearable.

God gave Moses strict instructions that no one was to touch that mountain—no one, not even an animal. If anyone so much as crossed the perimeter set around the mountain, they would be struck dead.

God then spoke to them out of the mountain, reminding them that they were a treasured possession to Him, and that

He had carried them on "eagles' wings" out of slavery unto Himself.

When the people saw this, here is how they responded: "All the people in the camp *trembled*... and they... "*believed*" (Exod. 19:16, author emphasis).

As a result of that belief, the Bible records in 19:8, and again in 24:3, that the people said, "All the words that the LORD has spoken we will do." Here is the progression: The people saw. The people believed. The people obeyed.

On that day they saw God's awesome size, His untouch-able holiness, and His tender mercy. That sight produced both a fear of God and faith in God. It was awe and wonder mingled with intimacy. The unap-proachable God was also their tender Father. Awe combined with intimacy is the essence of Christian worship. And then they pledged to obey.

> Awe combined with intimacy is the essence of Christian worship.

Really seeing those three things, God's awesome size, His untouchable holiness, and His tender mercy, is how we will change too.

God's awesome size

In the thunder and earthquakes and lightning, they saw that He was the God who commanded the magnificent pow-ers of creation.

There is something about awesome displays of nature that give you a glimpse of how big God is. Have you ever looked into the night sky and thought about how big the universe is? Astronomers tell us that if the distance between the sun and the earth were the thickness of one piece of paper, then the distance between the earth and the closest star would be a stack of paper 70 feet high. The distance across our galaxy would be a stack of paper 310 miles high. And our galaxy is but one of hundreds of thousands of galaxies in the known universe.

There is a God behind all of this who spoke it into existence with just a word and holds it all in the palm of His hand. The molecules obey His every word. Stars come into and out of existence at His whim.

He is so big that you literally cannot exaggerate Him. Awesome displays of nature—volcanoes, thunderstorms, sunsets, tornadoes, tsunamis—remind us of that.

The Israelites got a taste of that at the mountain.

I believe that most people today have lost a sense of God's awesome size. We reduce God to a domesticated, middle-class-sized deity that we can explain and control.

He is not. The infinite God staggers the mind. When we try to reduce God to someone we can explain and control, we actually cripple people's ability to believe in Him. Charles Misner, one of Einstein's students, explained that the reason Einstein never believed in the Christian God had a lot to do with how Christian preachers in his day spoke about God:

> The design of the universe is very magnificent and should not be taken for granted. In fact, I believe that is why Einstein had so little use for organized

religions, although he struck me as basically a very religious man. Einstein must have looked at what the preacher said about God and felt that they were blaspheming! He had seen more majesty than he had ever imagined in the creation of the universe and felt that the God they were talking about couldn't have been the real thing. My guess is that he simply felt that the churches he had run across did not have proper respect for the Author of the Universe.[1]

When we speak of God, we speak of One whose size and power and wisdom and might are far beyond our own. Perhaps one of the reasons we fail to treasure God is we have such a limited view of Him. God is a God of such massive size that our minds cease questioning when we see Him. We tremble and believe.

God's untouchable holiness

No one could touch the mountain, God said: "You cannot see my face . . . and live" (Exod. 33:20).

God is a God of such infinite perfection that not even the slightest sin in His presence can be tolerated. When Isaiah, the prophet of God, saw God upon His throne, he fell upon his face, terrified, and said, "Surely I am ruined, I have seen the Lord" (Isa. 6:5, author paraphrase). When Uzzah reached out his hand to steady the Ark of the Covenant where God's Spirit dwelled, he was struck dead.

God is a God whose holiness and perfection is so complete that sin cannot exist in His presence. I hear people often

speak glibly about "seeing God." If God ripped the roof off
the place where you were sitting right now and you saw His
face, you'd immediately die. Standing in the presence of God
with sin would be like a tissue paper touching the surface of
the sun.

Seeing and sensing God's holiness made Israel tremble.

We often think we have done God a favor by down-
playing the whole idea of His judgment. Our user-friendly
God does not punish sin. He certainly doesn't send people
to hell. But hell gives us a picture of the absolute perfection
and beauty of God. Hell is what hell is because God is who
God is. Hell is what hell is because that's what sin against an
infinitely beautiful and glorious God deserves. Hell is not one
degree hotter than our sin
demands that it be. Hell
should make our mouths
stand agape at the righ-
teous, just, holiness of
God.

> Hell is what hell is
> because that's what
> sin against an infinitely
> beautiful and glorious
> God deserves.

Have you ever heard
someone say that God
should not be "feared," only respected? You'd have a hard
time selling that to the Israelites after their encounter near
the mountain. That encounter was *designed* to produce fear.
It is only when we see the holiness of God—a sight that
should terrify us—that our hearts learn to worship Him. A
God that can satisfy our souls is a God that is so infinitely
beautiful that sin against Him requires severe and infinite
punishment.

Do you realize how completely pure and perfect God is? Do you realize what danger the presence of sin in your heart places you in? Imagine you were drinking a glass of milk and I told you it had been mixed with a few drops of human blood contaminated by the AIDS virus. That's not much, but touching that glass of milk to your lips would repulse you. We stand before God wholly contaminated by sin. Sin

> *True worship begins with fear. It doesn't end there, but that's where it starts.*

cannot exist in the presence of God. Israel had good reason to be afraid.

True worship begins with fear. It doesn't end there, but that's where it starts.

God's tender mercy

As Israel trembled before God's awesome size and absolute holiness, a voice spoke to them from the mountain, giving them these tender words:

> *"You have seen . . . how I bore you on eagles' wings and broiught you to myself. . . . [You are] my treasured posses-sion. . . . I am the LORD your God, who brought you out of the land of . . . slavery. (Exod. 19:4–5; 20:2)*

God says to them, "I saw your suffering and I heard your cries . . . I picked you up, tenderly, like a father would carry a wounded child out of a wreck and brought you to Myself."

There's an image I see frequently on the news that always moves me, whatever the context. The cameras are on the scene of some tragedy, and they'll capture some image of a father carrying the bloody, broken body of his child out of the wreckage. Maybe it's because I'm now a dad of four children, but seeing a father who has taken on his child's pain touches me somewhere deep in my soul.

> *There is only one word I can think of to describe God . . . beautiful.*

And I love that word *treasure.* God calls them His "treasured" possession. To treasure something means that you'd give up just about anything for it. If I found out my children had contracted some rare disease, and their only hope was an expensive medicine that insurance would not pay for, I would sell everything I had to get that medicine for them. Why? Because I treasure them.

The Mighty God of the universe, the God who has everything and lacks nothing, calls a helpless, guilty people His "treasure." He heard their cries, entered their pain, and rescued them.

There is only one word I can think of to describe a God so absolutely perfect that one sin in His presence leads to immediately annihilation yet so tender in His compassion that He enters into our pain rescue us: *beautiful.*

Sight Breaks the Power of Sin

Israel's response to this revelation was that they "believed" and they "trembled." They said, *"Whatever God says to us, we will do."* In light of what they'd seen, this is the God they wanted to know and obey.[2] They changed. Not just in their behavior, but in their *desires.* They wanted to know and obey God.

When we see the size and beauty of the God who speaks to us, the power of sin and idolatry over our hearts is broken.

The way that we will stop sinning is not by being told over and over, "Stop sinning!" but by seeing the majesty and glory of God in our hearts.

"But wait!" you might say. "The Bible is full of directives and prohibitions. Isn't the point of the Bible to stop sinning?"

Yes. But ceasing sin is the *by-product* of seeing God. As we see the beauty of God and feel His weightiness in our hearts, our hearts begin to desire Him more than we desire sin. Before the Bible says, "Stop sinning," it says, *"Behold your God!"*

Think of it like a balloon. There are two ways to keep a balloon afloat. If you fill a balloon with your breath, then the only way to keep it in the air is to continually smack it upward. That's how religion keeps you motivated: it repeatedly "hits" you. "Stop doing this!" "Get busy with that!" This is my life as a pastor. People come on a Sunday so I can "smack" them about something. "Be more generous!" And they do that for a week. "Go do missions!" And they sign up for a trip. Every week I smack them back into spiritual orbit. No wonder people don't like being around me.

But there's another way to keep a balloon afloat. Fill it with helium. Then it floats on its own, no smacking required. Seeing the size and beauty of God is like the helium that keeps us soaring spiritually.

When you have seen the beauty of God and felt the weightiness of God's majesty in your soul, sin's power over you will be broken. I often tell college-aged guys at our church that they can turn their sexual drives on and off like a light switch. They never believe me. I tell them, "I'll prove it to you . . . Imagine that you are alone with your girlfriend, sitting with her on the couch at her house. Your sexual desires begin to take over and you feel like there is no way you can turn them off. At that moment, you feel totally out of control, like there is no way to say 'no' to the power of temptation." They say, "Exactly." I tell them, "At just that moment, her Army Ranger father walks in. . . . See? Sexual desire, off like a light switch!"

> *When you have seen the beauty of God and felt the weightiness of God's majesty in your soul, sin's power over you will be broken.*

Where did it go? It is not that they suddenly lost libido, it was just that in that moment their fear of her Ranger father was weightier to them than the sexual lust. Desire for her was surpassed by a desire to avoid death.

The reason many of us feel like we "can't say no" to temptations is that God does not have that kind of weight in our hearts. God's authority must be greater than our desires; His beauty should be more attractive than any lust of the flesh. In other words, the reason we can't say no to temptation is not that our desires for those things is too large; it's because our desire for God is too small.

In order to really say no to the desires of temptation, we need to develop a stronger desire for God. Lesser urges can only be expelled by stronger ones. Puritan Thomas Chalmers called this "the expulsive power of a new affection." Our affections for idols are brought under control only when they are taken captive by a stronger, more enchanting affection.

> *Our affections for idols are brought under control only when they are taken captive by a stronger, more enchanting affection.*

Until that happens, all changes we make will be superficial. We will obey only when we think there is a threat of punishment or the promise of reward. This kind of obedience is wearisome, both to God and to us. We are forcing our hearts to pursue what they don't want to pursue.

Most people live in a dual-captivity: they are captive to the sinful lusts of their heart; but they are also captive to the rules of their religion. Sin makes them desire the wrong thing; their religion keeps them from doing what they now desire. Seeing the glory of God revealed in the gospel gives us freedom from both sin and religion. The gospel sets us free from the threat of condemnation and changes our hearts so that we want to know and serve God.

You say, "But wait! If people think that Christ has already taken all the penalty for their sin and no threat of punishment remains, then they will do whatever they want."

Well, at least now we're asking the right question. This is exactly the objection Paul expected after laying out the gospel in Romans 1–5. His answer: if people only want to pursue sin, that reveals that their hearts are spiritually dead (Rom. 6:1–2). The answer is not, Paul says, to slap rules on them. If your heart loves sin, throw yourself on the mercy of God, asking Him to change your heart and embrace His righteousness given to you as a gift. Only then will your heart change. The goodness of God, Paul says, is what produces real repentance in us (Rom. 2:4).

Freedom from sin, you see, is *hating* sin. As the early church father Ignatius said: "It is impossible for a man (truly) to be freed from the habit of sin before he hates it." You will only hate sin when you start to love God. You learn to love God by seeing His beauty and love for you revealed in the gospel.

The leaders of the church had placed John Bunyan, the author of *Pilgrim's Progress*, in prison for preaching the gospel. They told him, "You can't go on telling people that Christ's righteousness has been credited to them in full. If they believe that, they'll feel like they can do whatever they want!" Bunyan replied, "If people really see that Christ's righteousness has been given to them entirely as a gift, they'll do whatever *He* wants."

"So, where can *we* see God?"

"So," you say, "Where can we see God like that? Where's our mountain where God descends before us in fire?"

Good question. I'm not telling you to break out Cecil B. DeMille's *Ten Commandments* and watch it over and over. The mountain in Exodus 19, as impressive as it was, was just a dim shadow of a later mountain where God's glory would be revealed—Mount Calvary. More than 1,400 years after God appeared on Mount Sinai, Jesus would climb up another mountain to put God's glory on display. Just like Sinai, Calvary was covered by a thick cloud of darkness as God turned His face away. On the cross Jesus would endure the thunder of God's judgment and absorb the lightning of His wrath into His body. The fire of God's holiness

> The gospel not only tells us about the power of God; the message of the gospel is itself the power of God.

would burn through the body of Christ until it completely consumed Him. We transgressed the lines of God's holiness, and Jesus was struck dead for it. When Jesus died, the earth literally shook, and the last thing Jesus would do from the cross is yell, with a voice like a trumpet, "*It is finished!*"

The burning mountain of Exodus 19 was a picture of Mount Calvary, where Jesus gave us the clearest and most complete picture of the glory of God.

In the cross we see the magnanimity of God's grace. God did more than carry us on eagles' wings from danger;

He rescued us out of the jaws of death by substituting Himself in our place. Imagine standing about a half mile from the Hoover Dam, that massive structure holding back untold amounts of water. Imagine, to your horror, that you suddenly saw a crack forming up from the bottom of the dam, only to see a massive force of water burst through the dam and a wave five hundred feet high come rushing down the valley toward you. Death is certain. But suddenly, right before the water sweeps you away, the ground in front of you opens up and swallows every ounce, so that not a drop touches you. When Jesus died on the cross, He stood between us and the rushing river of God's righteous wrath. He swallowed up every ounce into Himself, so that not a drop remains for you or me. He drank the cup of God's wrath to its dregs, turned it over, and said, "It is finished."

He did that for you because you are a treasure to Him.

In the cross we see the massiveness of God's power. The gospel reveals a greater power than even the power of creation. It is the power of new creation; redeeming from sin and regenerating life from death. Paul calls the gospel "the power of God" (Rom. 1:16). Did you know that nothing else in Scripture, except for Christ Himself, is referred to directly as "the power of God"? Think about that—the sun is 9,900 degrees Farenheit on the surface and 27 million degrees at its core. Tsunami waves rise up to 100 feet high and travel at over 80 miles an hour, destroying everything in their path. A recently discovered star is reported to streak through the heavens at 1.5 million miles per hour. We know of volcanoes that spew lava up to 17 miles into the atmosphere and whose eruptions can be heard more than 3,000 miles away.[3] One human DNA strand, invisible to the human eye, contains enough information to fill one thousand 500-page books. None of those is called "the power of God." Jesus' victorious work of putting away our sin forever and rising triumphant over the grave, however, is what God calls "My power."

> *Believing the gospel is not only the way we become Christians, it is the power that enables us to do, every moment of every day, the very things Jesus commands us to do.*

As you see and believe that gospel, its power is actually released into you. You see, the gospel not only tells us about the power of God; the message of the gospel is *itself* the power of God. By the power of the Spirit, the hearing of the gospel re-creates our hearts to love the things God commands. Think of it like Jesus' command to the lame man to walk. When Jesus said, "Rise, take up your bed, and walk," He was giving the lame man not only a command, but His words also gave the power to obey that command. In the same way the gospel God gives the power to do what He commands.

Believing the gospel is not only the way we become Christians, it is the power that enables us to do, every moment of every day, the very things Jesus commands us to do.

Mahmud's Vision

One night while I was living in an Islamic country I received a phone call from a man I had never met named Mahmud. Mahmud explained to me that he had had a very important dream, and he believed that I was supposed to help him interpret it. In his dream he had wandered aimlessly in an endless field. This field, he told me, seemed to him to symbolize his life. He felt alone, without purpose, true companionship or direction. After walking for what seemed like days, he heard a voice behind him call his name. There he saw a man who, in his words, "was dressed in shining white clothing. I could not look on his face, because it shone like the sun." This heavenly man reached into the sash of his robe and pulled out a copy of the gospel and tried to place it in Mahmud's hands. "This," the man said to Mahmud, calling him by name, "will get you out of this field."

Mahmud refused. Mahmud was a faithful Muslim, and he had no desire to possess "Christian literature." He woke up in a cold sweat, heart beating quickly, and feeling very afraid. He said he felt as if he had rejected a prophet and did not know what to do.

When he fell asleep the second night, he found himself again in the field. Again, the "man" appeared, offering Mahmud another copy of the gospel. And again Mahmud refused.

The third night when Mahmud went to sleep, the man was there waiting on him. "This, and only this," he said to Mahmud, "will get you out of this field." With trembling hand, Mahmud took the gospel from the man.

Mahmud then said to me, "My friend tells me that you are an expert in the gospel. Can you interpret my dream for me?" No joke. That is what he said.

Now, I was raised in a very traditional Baptist home, and dreams or visions were not part of our standard religious repertoire. So, I said, "Mahmud, I don't believe in visions and dreams."

Not really. I looked at him and said, "Brother, you are so in luck, dream interpretation just happens to be my spiritual gift."

For the next two hours I explained the gospel to him. Though he still had questions, he didn't really doubt the answers I was giving him. After all, he'd been instructed by a divine messenger to listen! When I explained to him how Jesus had taken his sin on the cross, he said, with tears streaming down his face, "Allah . . . the Creator God, dying in my place? Can this be true? Oh, *Allahu Akbar, Allahu Akbar*" (What Muslims say when they give praise to God—meaning, literally, God is the greatest!).

It was obvious he had believed, so I asked him if he would like to place His faith in Jesus. When he said yes, I asked him if he knew what such commitment might cost him. "Mahmud," I said, "you might lose your job. You might get kicked out of your family. This commitment to Christ might even cost you your life."

I'll never forget what he said next. He smiled and said, "Of course I know all that. That is why it took me over a month to come talk with you, because I knew that if I became a follower of Jesus it might cost me everything . . . but if Jesus Christ is God, and God gave Himself like that for me on the cross, I will go anywhere with Him. If I lose my job, my family, or my life, it is OK. I'd go with Jesus anywhere."

You may never have had a "vision" of Jesus in your dreams like that. I haven't either. While our experience may not be that dramatic, our response to Jesus should be no less total. We see the glory of God, Paul says, in the face of Jesus Christ presented to us in the Gospels. What we see there is better than a dream or vision. Becoming a follower of Jesus means having your heart so enraptured by the beauty, majesty, and value of God's gift of Himself to you that knowing and pleasing Him becomes the one driving passion of your heart. Even if it costs you everything else.

What about You?

Do you feel the weight of God's majesty in your soul in this way? You may have read the Bible a thousand times, but have you ever been so overwhelmed at the display of God's power and glory that you tremble? Before Christianity tells you to *do* anything, it calls you to sit in wonder and amazement at what God has done *for you*.

> Get down on your knees, open the pages of the Gospels, and pray that the Jesus who walks through the pages of Matthew, Mark, Luke, and John gives you a glimpse of His true majesty.

Is your heart captivated by the glory and beauty of God? Are you overcome by a sense of awe *and* drawn in by a feeling of intimacy? If not, why not get down on your knees right now and beg God to open the eyes of your heart to let you see Him for who He really is? Better yet, why not get down on your knees, open the pages of the Gospels, and pray that the Jesus who walks through the pages of Matthew, Mark, Luke, and John gives you a glimpse of His true majesty? You'll never be the same. And you'll find yourself saying these words over and over again, now with your whole heart:

*"Your presence and approval are all
I need for everlasting joy."*

CHAPTER 7

Gospel-Centered Relationships

What is the one, definitive mark of those who have been saved? Growing up, I heard lots of answers to that question. At one church I visited, they said that if you were really saved, you would show it by (a) a change in your language; (b) the way you dressed (if you were a boy, you took out your earrings, cut your hair short, and wore pleated khakis); (c) a sudden and intense hatred for beer, cigarettes, and Disney; and (d) a preference for music with little to no drumbeat.

Most of that is ridiculous. But the gospel does bring an unmistakable change in your life.

The third part of The Gospel Prayer is,

"As You have been to me, so I will be to others."

It's impossible to really experience the grace of the gospel and not be transformed into a person of kindness, generosity, and love. When we experience the generosity of the gospel, we will naturally extend that generosity to others. We become people with a generous spirit, and that affects how we treat others and what we do with our money, time, and talents.

Grace and Victor Hugo

One of my all-time favorite movie scenes is the opening sequence in the 1998 movie rendition of Victor Hugo's *Les Misérables*. Liam Neeson plays the part of Jean Valjean, a bitter criminal who has just been paroled from a hard-labor camp in France.

He stumbles alone late one night to the home of a priest, who invites him in and offers him food and shelter for the evening. That night Valjean steals all the silverware in the priest's home. The priest, hearing some commotion in his house, gets up to investigate. Valjean punches him in the face and knocks him out. He then leaves with the stolen silver.

Early the next morning the police drag Valjean back to the home of the priest. The guard mockingly says to the priest, "He told us you gave this silver to him!" Being a paroled prisoner, all the priest has to do is confirm that Valjean stole the silverware, and Valjean will go back to prison—for life.

The priest, his face still bruised and bloodied from the night before, looks at Valjean and says, "Why yes. Yes, I did. I'm very angry with you, Jean Valjean . . ." Then he adds, unexpectedly, '. . . because you forgot the candlesticks. Why did you forget the candlesticks? They are worth almost 2,000 francs."

The guard immediately orders Valjean to be released. Valjean, meanwhile, is dumbfounded at the turn of events. The priest knew he stole the silver, and Valjean knew the priest knew. And yet the priest not only vouched for the convict, he shoved additional wealth into his sack. In explanation the priest says quietly to Valjean: "And now don't you forget it. Don't you ever forget it. You've promised to become a new man. "Jean Valjean, my brother, you no longer belong to evil. With this silver I've bought your soul. I've ransomed you from fear and hatred . . . and now I give you back to God."

Les Misérables is the story of how Valjean becomes "the new man" the priest declared he would become. The mercy of the priest transforms Valjean from a hardened criminal into a patient, kind, generous man who cares for the poor and the orphan. A recipient of great mercy, he becomes a giver of great mercy.

This, of course, is not the full gospel. It takes more than an act of mercy to change our hearts. The Spirit of God has to open our eyes to the mercy and beauty of God in Christ and give us a desire for it. But there is truth in Hugo's central point: mercy begets mercy.

Hugo had a wealth of material to draw from in the Gospels when he crafted his tale. In Matthew 18:23–25, for example, Jesus told a story about one man who owed another man an extraordinary amount of money—"ten thousand talents" to be specific. (That's a lot of money. Think "Congressional stimulus package.") The day came when the debt was due, and the man was called in to account. The man couldn't pay and consequently was sentenced to "debtor's prison." There he would labor, together with his family, until the debt was paid off—even if it meant subsequent generations remained imprisoned.

The man, hopeless, threw himself on the ground and began to plead for mercy—more time to pay off the debt. Everyone watching this pathetic scene began to feel uncomfortable, because loan officers don't become successful by showing mercy. They're not called "loan bunnies" or "loan puppies"; they are called "loan sharks." If you don't pay, someone named Bruno shows up at your house to break your thumbs.

But then the most unexpected thing happened. This loan shark felt an emotion Jesus calls *"splagma,"* a Greek word meaning a gut-level compassion for the guy. We don't know why. Perhaps he remembered his own children, or maybe he just identified with this guy—whatever—and his bottom lip started to quiver and a tear filled his eye. He then said the unthinkable: "Forget about it. You owe me nothing."

No one in the room could believe it, least of all the forgiven man. For the first time in his life, he felt free. He thanked the loan officer profusely and emerged from the courtroom a new man. He rushed home, feeling light as air, to tell his family the news of their release.

As he crossed the street across from the courthouse, he saw an old colleague who owed him $3. He grabbed the man by the neck and said, "Give me my $3." The guy said, "I'm sorry. I've had a bad week. I don't have any money. I'll pay you next week." "No!" the man shrieked. "If you can't pay now, you're going to prison."

I imagine that when Jesus was telling this story, at this point His hearers rolled their eyes. "Give me a break. *Nobody* forgiven of millions of dollars would throw someone in prison over $3." And that is Jesus' point *exactly*. There is no way you could have any concept of what God has forgiven you of

> Those people who really believe the gospel become like the gospel.

and be ungenerous in spirit toward others. If you are, it must mean you are unaware of the grace God as shown toward you.

Those people who really believe the gospel show it by becoming like the gospel.

Someone saturated in the grace of the gospel develops an almost insane ability to forgive.

A Radical Forgiveness

It was my failure to grasp the grace shown to me in the gospel that almost destroyed my marriage.

My wife and I have been married for eight *wonderful* years. Plus two other ones, for a total of ten. Those first two years were rough. I remember my wife and I crooning to each other a few months before we got married, "We never fight—we must be perfect for each other!" And we didn't fight. At that point. Throughout the entire year of our dating relationship and engagement, I cannot remember a single altercation.

Well, we made up for lost time during the first six months of our marriage.

After grueling it out for a couple of years, in desperation we went to see a biblical counselor. He opened his Bible to

1 Timothy 1:15 where Paul describes himself as the "chief" of sinners (NKJV). He then asked us if we thought Paul was exaggerating when he called himself that. My doctrine of the Bible made me want to say "no," since the Bible is inerrant and Paul doesn't exaggerate. But how could Paul *really* think he was a bigger sinner than Judas Iscariot or Nero?

Still completely unaware of where the counselor was going with this, I said, "I don't know."

He said that Paul was indeed telling the truth in saying that because in his perception, he was the biggest sinner. Paul was better acquainted with his own sinfulness than he was anyone else's. Of course Paul knew, theoretically, that other people were every bit the sinner he was, but he was so much more aware of his sin than he was theirs. When Paul thought about a need for grace, he didn't think of others first—he thought of himself.

Our counselor explained that both my wife and I saw *one another, and not ourselves,* as "the chief of sinners." I could see my wife's sin, but I was blissfully oblivious to my own. If I had understood my own deep need for grace, I would have more naturally extended grace to her.

The counselor's next words exploded in my heart like a bombshell: "When you really believe the gospel, you see that you are first a sinner and only secondarily sinned against. The problem in your marriage is that neither of you seems aware of how much you've been forgiven. Because you haven't really tasted grace, you won't extend grace to each other. You need to go back to the gospel."

Our marriage problems were gospel problems. That afternoon my wife and I began to explore more intimately the grace that had been extended to us in Christ. Through that study our entire disposition toward one another changed. We began to see ourselves as first, sinner, and second, sinned against; and as we became more aware of our own need for grace, we became more willing to extend it to each other.

We still hurt and disappoint one another. We still get impatient. But when I think about how much God has forgiven me of, what I'm asked to forgive her of doesn't seem that substantial. As we stand amazed at what God has done for us in the cross of Christ, we find it hard to stay angry at one another.

As God's grace changes us, our grace changes others

In having dealt with a number of struggling marriages in our church over the years, I have noticed that one of the biggest obstacles to showing grace to others is the belief that if you do not retaliate, those who hurt you will never learn the wrongness of what they have done. We take it upon ourselves to educate our spouses, our kids, our coworkers, our parents, and anyone else in our path as to their faults and how they've hurt us.

That's what I thought during those first two years of marriage. I thought the only way really to change my wife was to make her feel the pain of what she was doing to me. If I hurt her in the same way she hurt me, she'd repent.

> God changed us by pouring out undeserved kindness on us.

Furthermore, I felt right in paying her back for her wrong. When we are wronged, a little divine tuning fork rings in our hearts telling us that the balance of justice in the universe is off. We feel nigh unto deity when we are righting the wrong. We think when we restore the balance of justice, everyone will start behaving properly again.

That is a lie. Is that how God changed us, by punishing us for our sin? No. God changed us by pouring out undeserved kindness on us. When we tasted that, our hearts were transformed.

We will help others change in the exact same way. Paul explained it this way:

> *Beloved, never avenge yourselves, but leave it to the wrath of God, for it is written, "Vengeance is mine, I will repay, says the Lord." To the contrary, "if your enemy is hungry, feed him; if he is thirsty, give him something to drink; for by so doing you will heap burning coals on his head." Do not be overcome by evil, but overcome evil with good. (Rom. 12:19–21)*

My favorite phrase in that verse is that by returning good for evil we will *"heap burning coals on [our enemy's] head."* That sounds like what I wanted to do to my enemy (um . . . my wife) in the first place! But Paul isn't saying that we dump coals on someone's head to *hurt* them—that, after all, would be against the entire spirit of this passage. Dumping coals on their head is meant *to wake them up.*

The person who receives your kindness in response to their sin is shocked into awareness. Your kindness to them makes them see the absurdity of their selfishness and helps awaken them to the blessings of relationship.

Only then, Paul says, will you *overcome* evil. You can't overcome evil in someone by paying them back. You'll only perpetuate it. Your retaliation will produce more anger in them, and, in turn, more evil, if not toward you, toward someone else. You destroy the evil in someone by showing them extravagant grace.

Jesus said it this way: when we are wronged, we should "turn the other cheek." Some interpret that to mean that we engage in some type of unrealistic pacifism. Someone punches us in the face, and we stand back up, look at them and say, "Is that all you got? I'm still standing! Here, hit me again!"

But in Jewish thought, the "cheek" was the symbol of relationship; kissing someone's cheek was the sign of peace and fellowship. "Striking someone's cheek" meant that you are attacking the relationship. To have your cheek struck meant that friends were taking you for granted. Not giving you respect. Talking behind your back. Not thinking about your needs.

Jesus says, "Turn your other cheek to them." In other words, *reoffer the relationship* to them. Jesus did not say "turn the same cheek back to them," as in "let them hit you again." Nor did he say "strike them on their cheek in return," as in, "retaliate so they are in pain too." He said "turn the other cheek" *to* them.[1] Reoffer the blessings of relationship. We might need to confront them where they wronged us, but we do so without the slightest desire to wound in return. We absorb the sting of their blow and offer them the kindness of a restored relationship.

Just like Jesus did for us.

In confronting them, you are not trying to verbally pay them back for their offense—verbally whipping them. You are confronting them for *their sake*, because you are saddened by what their sin is doing to them, and what it is doing to your relationship. You do this in love, more concerned with how their sin is hurting them rather than its effect on you. Where they were selfish and cruel, you respond with tenderness and a desire to reconcile. You absorb their violence and offer them peace. By so doing you might very well "awaken" them out of their destructive behavior.

The gospel does not tell us to be passive toward others in their faults. It tells us to be aggressively graceful. We overcome evil with good. "Overcome" is a warrior's term. Paul is saying, "Go to war with evil, and defeat it soundly with grace."

> The gospel does not tell us to be passive toward others in their faults. It tells us to be aggressively graceful. We overcome evil with good.

Jesus overcame evil in us through the grace of the cross. We will overcome evil in others by being to them as Jesus was to us.

Men, we are supposed to lead in this in our marriages. When Paul tells us to "love our wives like Christ loves the church," this is primarily what he was talking about. Christ loved the church by receiving her hurtful blows and offering her only love in response. His grace toward the church did not find, but made, the church beautiful. This produced in the church a love for Him that could never have been produced through retaliation. C. S. Lewis said it well: "This verse [Eph. 5:25] is most embodied in the husband whose wife receives most and gives the least, it's the one whose wife is most unworthy of him, is—in her own mere nature—least lovable. For the church has no beauty but what the bridegroom gives her; he does not find, but makes her, lovely."[2] We make our wives beautiful by extending to them the grace of the cross. This "washes them with the word," and helps form in them Christ-like character. Christ did it for us, first; we do it for our wives, second.

We respond to God, not to others

Now, I hear what you might be saying. "But this person does not *deserve* my grace. You don't know how deeply they've hurt me."

As compassionately as I can, I want to tell you: *That's the whole point.*

We didn't deserve God's grace when God saved us, either. The bottom line is that the person we choose to forgive may not change when we first show them grace. We didn't either. I don't know many people who believed the gospel the first time they heard it. Jesus extended grace to me a long time before I changed. He died for me "while I was still a sinner" (Rom. 5:8).

In fact, the person you are forgiving might never change. And that's OK, because forgiveness has a benefit to forgive, too. We get a chance to love like God loves. Even if showing grace never changes those we forgive, it changes us, and that is God's primary purpose in all that is happening to us in this life. Paul says God is working *all* things in our lives together toward His good plan of conforming us to the image of His Son (Rom. 8:28–29).

Ultimately I am responding to Jesus, not to the person in front of me. The person wronging me may not deserve a response of grace, but the Jesus who bled and died for me does.

So . . . you're waiting for the repairman, who is two hours late. When he comes in you want to go Old Testament on him. Perhaps in that moment of frustration you might remember, "This repairman's tardiness is nothing compared to the blasphemy I committed against God." You might still confront the repairman about his tardiness, but you'll have an entirely different spirit. (Note: This has happened to me a lot. I have become aware that God seems to have appointed a whole army of incompentent, uncaring people for my sanctification.)

> When you have tasted the grace of the gospel, no relationship, no matter how wrong or hurtful or annoying, looks the same to you.

When you have tasted the grace of the gospel, no relationship, no matter how wrong or hurtful or annoying, looks the same to you. You'll see yourself as "first, sinner, and second, sinned against," and when that happens, your entire disposition toward others' offenses toward you will change.

The clearest mark of God's grace in your life is a generous spirit toward others.

You should daily think on the grace of God shown you in Christ, and pray:

"As You have been to me, so I will be to others."

CHAPTER 8

Extravagant Generosity

"As you have been to me so I will be to others."

That's the mantra of a grace-soaked believer. We've seen how that creates in us a generous spirit toward the offenses of others. But how does that change our attitude toward our possessions? What does a gospel-centered believer's relationship with money look like?

I know you're probably expecting a pretty pat answer here. Something like, "Whatever you're giving . . . it's not enough. There are kids in India who survive on three grains of rice a day. Feel guilty and give more."

Understanding the gospel will certainly lead you to extravagant generosity. How could it not? "You know the grace of our Lord Jesus Christ" Paul says, "that though he was rich, yet for your sake he became poor, so that you by his poverty might become rich" (2 Cor. 8:9). If we understand what Jesus gave up to save us, how could we not willingly and joyfully give up our possessions so that others might have life also?

But there is a dilemma. How could we ever give up enough to equal what Jesus gave up for us? Jesus had His beloved Father turn His face away from Him in the hour He needed Him most. None of us will ever give up anything that even compares to that.

In addition to that, the Bible talks about a number of things God wants us to do with our money besides just give it away (though He certainly does want us to be extravagantly generous with it). Money is a tool He puts in our hands for the accomplishing multiple purposes in our lives. So, this chapter is a little more of an in-depth look on what "gospel-centered generosity" looks like.[1]

Two Primary Errors

I find that there are two primary errors when it comes to Christians' attitudes toward giving.

The first error goes something like this:

"God wants 10 percent, and after that you can do whatever you want with your money."

In other words, after you've tithed, you've done your duty, so you can go on your merry way using the other 90 percent to lavish gifts upon yourself. For many Christians giving away that first 10 percent is actually means to getting God to increase the other 90 percent. "Bring the tithe into the storehouse," they say, "and see if God will not open up the windows of heaven and pour out such an abundance of blessing that you cannot contain it" (Mal. 3:10, author paraphrase).

For these believers, giving is an investment plan to get more stuff.

This position, by itself, is not just incomplete—it is more *unChristian*, because, ultimately, its primary motivation is money. We give to God to get more money from God. It is true that God promises to bless us when we give, but receiving more money is not the primary reason we are to give. We should give in grateful response to a God who gave everything for us. When we give to God primarily in order to get more from Him, we are not worshipping God; we are *using* Him (2 Cor. 8:6; 9:8; 1 Tim. 6:6).

This kind of giving has nothing to do with what Jesus was talking about when He said to "take up our cross" and follow Him. Following Jesus means that we leverage our lives for the kingdom of God, just as He leveraged His for us. Jesus said His life was like a seed that fell into the ground and died so that life could come out of it to benefit others. Every disciple of Jesus must feel the same about his or her own life (John 12:24). Jesus did not tithe His blood for us, He gave it all. What He deserves in response—indeed, what He demands—is a full offering of our lives.

> Jesus said His life was like a seed that fell into the ground and died so that life could come out of it to benefit others.

Those people who give God a tithe so they can get on with a self-centered life have not yet embraced the path of discipleship.

The second, and opposite, error in Christian approaches to giving goes something like this:

"The only thing you should do with your money is give it away to the poor. After all, there are always more poor and more lost people. Thus, if there's something you have that you could give away and still survive, you should give it away."

I've heard this attitude toward our possessions described before as a "battle" mentality. In a battle, you divest yourself of all luxuries to provide resources for the battle. All your "luxury metal" gets melted town for bullets. All available capital should therefore be used to feed the poor and pay the salaries of missionaries.

Remember that scene in *Schindler's List* when the reality of how many Jews had been killed in the Holocaust sets in on Liam Neeson and he looks at his watch and says, "This watch . . . I didn't need this watch. Why couldn't I have sold this? This watch could have freed two Jews . . ." That's how people in this position think.

This position suggests that we should live as minimally as humanly possible and give all the rest away. You ask questions like this:

• "If your kids were starving, wouldn't you liquidate your retirement to feed them?"

- "If your children were sold in the sex trade, wouldn't you give up everything you had to rescue them?"

I find this position inspiring, and it is certainly at least partially correct (we are in a real battle with real casualties and we can't ignore that). But while this position is much more in line with the New Testament than the previous approach, it is still out of balance with the full biblical teaching on money, and in places with the gospel itself.

I advocated this position personally for a while, and, quite honestly, it led me to despair. There was always someone else who needed Jesus and another orphan to be cared for. So, did I really need to get a Coke with lunch? Couldn't I drink tap water and give that $1.40 to missions? Wouldn't that feed an orphan for a week? Or, should I ever be eating out at all? And even if I eat at home, can I eat anything above beans and rice? Lots of orphans don't even have that. And do I really need a wedding ring—or, at the very least, a gold one? I could sell my one gold ring and give that money to missions. Were the curtains in my house a peacetime luxury that should really go to provide warm pajamas for a kid in India?

Correcting Our Perspective

I have come to see four biblical errors with that attitude:
First, this kind of thinking has no practical end. When is enough, enough? As I mentioned at the beginning of this chapter, if a person compares their sacrifice to that of Jesus, they will always come up short. He left heaven to come to earth, had no place to lay His head, and died a torturous

death. He faced abandonment by God. There's nothing we can do to equal the sacrifice of Jesus.

As to the battle mentality . . . well, in battle, if I had no bullets and the enemy was coming for my family, I would melt down *all* my spoons and eat with my hands so I could have bullets to defend my kids. I have noticed, however, that most proponents of the give-it-all-away view, however, still have spoons. Do they really care more about their precious spoons than they do lost souls in the Sudan? If not, why not sell their spoons? Surely they could survive without spoons!

Sincere believers advocating this position tell us to "spend money only on necessities; give away any excess." But what exactly is *excess*? If you ate anything above rice and beans, wasn't that excess?

Five hundred years ago John Calvin perceived the never-ending trajectory of this type of thinking. He said,

> If a man begins to doubt whether he may use linen for his sheets, shirts, handkerchiefs, and napkins, he will afterward be uncertain also about hemp . . . For he will turn over in his mind whether he can sup without napkins, or go without handkerchief. If any man should consider daintier food unlawful, in the end he will not be at peace before God, when he eats either black bread or common victuals, while it occurs to him that he could sustain his body on even coarser foods. If he boggles at sweet wine, he will not with clear conscience drink even flat wine, and finally he will not dare touch water if sweeter and cleaner than other water."[2]

Second, this approach assumes that God needs our money.
This should come as no surprise to you, but He does not.
God created the world with just a word and no help from any
of us. He can make enough food for 5,000 families with just
five loaves and two fish. He can use the "two mites" of the
widow to do more than the richest of the rich. He can make
money appear in fish's mouths when He needs it. Whenever
He so desires, He can persuade a King Cyrus to pay for the
rebuilding of Jerusalem. Believe me, He's not short on money.
He owns the cattle on a thousand hills and can sell any of
them whenever He wants. At no point does He ever approach
us as if He *needs* on our resources to get His job done.

That's not to say that He hasn't made the church
co-laborers in His mission. It is certainly true that He has put
into the hands of the church the material resources He plans
to use to bring salvation to the world. But while God uses our
generosity as part of His plan, that's different than implying
that God needs our money to get the job done.

*Third, this position ends up being, for all its spiritualized
language, a form of "compulsory" giving.* We are racked by guilt
and give to alleviate it. Gospel-centered giving, by contrast, is
characterized by freedom. We give in joyful response to the
grace of Christ because there is nothing we'd rather do with
our money than glorify Him and see His kingdom come on
the earth.

The New Testament goes to meticulous lengths to avoid
prescribing an amount believers should give. For example,
in the gospel of Luke, at least three times Jesus commends a
different amount.

- In Luke 18:22 Jesus is talking to a rich young ruler who has tons of money and Jesus says to him, "Give away *all* of your money—every penny! And come and follow me."
- In Luke 11, Jesus is referring to how some people give and He says, "You tithe" (which is giving away 10 percent) and He says, "This is good" (Luke 11:42).
- Here in Luke 19:9 Zacchaeus gives away 50 percent and Jesus says, "That is very good and proves you've been saved."

For type A people like me, such ambiguity drives us crazy. "Well, which is it, Jesus? Is it 100 percent? Or 10 percent? Or 50 percent? Jesus, I need a box to check off. What's the exact amount I have to give to get 'the gold star'?"

The point is, *there is no one answer* . . . a spirit of generosity is simply not something you can produce by establishing a standard.

Fourth, this position is out of sync with a number of other things the Bible teaches about God's purpose in giving us possessions. God did not give us money simply for us to give it away. Please don't misinterpret that. God does provide us with a lot of money that He does indeed want us to leverage for others—to give it away freely. But God has other purposes in giving us money beyond giving it away. According to Paul, God gives us some material things to enjoy and He is glorified as we enjoy them. Any good father loves to delight his children with gifts; our Heavenly Father is no different. Wise King Solomon taught us that saving money can be prudent, and that godly men often leave money even to their children's children. So let's delve more into what those purposes are.

The Generosity Matrix

We like rules, formulas, and black-and-white prescriptions. With money, however, the Bible gives us complementary values a gospel-centered heart holds in balance.

I find at least six biblical principles about money that we should hold in reverent tension. *Any one of these principles, taken alone, will knock you out of balance.* Holding all six principles in tension, however, leads you to extravagant generosity and humble appreciation of God's good gifts. Here they are!

1. God gives excess to some so that they can share with those who have less.

In 2 Corinthians 8:13–15, Paul uses the story of the manna given to the Israelites in the wilderness to explain God gives excess to some so we can share it with others. If my wife packs my little girl's lunch, and she put two sandwiches in it because she knew there was a kid at school who had nothing, we would want her to give it away when she was given the chance. We don't need her to squirrel it away in case tomorrow we forget to give her lunch. We won't forget. God does the same with us. He gives excess to some of us today so we can share today with those in need today. He won't forget about us tomorrow.

The Old Testament talks in numerous places about believers' responsibility to the poor. James says that if we see a brother suffering and withhold our resources from him, then we are not really people of faith. Acts says in that early church "there was not a needy person among them, for as many as were owners of lands or houses sold them and brought the proceeds of what was sold and laid it at the apostles' feet, and it was distributed to each as any had need" (Acts 4:34–35).

> Those of us with relatively a lot should give freely to those with little. It's precisely why God gave some of us a lot.

Thus, those of us with relatively a lot should give freely to those with little. It's precisely *why* God gave some of us a lot. We'll have to answer to Him for what we do with our abundance. Sharing with the poor is both our duty and our joyful privilege.[3]

2. Jesus' radical generosity toward us serves as a model and a motivation for our radical generosity.

In 2 Corinthians 8–9. Paul further explains to the Corinthians that Jesus' generosity toward them should be the pattern of their generosity toward others.

As I said above, Jesus did not merely tithe His blood; He gave all of it. As God increases our ability to earn money and gives us greater positions of power, we should leverage that power and money like Jesus did—not to increase our standard of living, but to increase our standard of giving. We should think of life like Jesus did, Paul says, who leveraged His position and His resources to save us rather than prosper Himself. Thus, we should leverage our prosperity for the sake of world evangelization, not greater self-indulgence. Paul says that God actually multiplies our financial resources *for the purpose of* increasing our "seed for sowing" (2 Cor. 9:10).

How can any of us who have tasted the extravagant love of Christ be stingy with our resources? Doesn't His compassion toward us make us naturally disposed to help those in need? If we see someone who has a need that we can meet, how can our heart not want to help them? Won't we love the fatherless, and the widow, and the shut-in, and the homeless, since we know that we once were fatherless, estranged from the Father, disabled, and headed for eternal separation from God?

How can we say we love others and not pour out our lives so that others can hear? I was once sharing the gospel with a girl named Rhonda. After talking for quite some time, she said, "I couldn't believe what you believe. It would wreck my life." I said, "Why?" She said, "If I believed what you believed— that my friends were condemned and salvation could only be found by believing in Jesus—I would approach each of them—in fact, every person I met—on my hands and knees and *plead* with them to believe in Jesus. I would never stop pleading, never stop weeping, until I had convinced everyone to believe." Do we feel that way about the lost?

Paul, who talked so much about freedom in the Christian life, says he

> *As God increases our ability to earn money and gives us greater positions of power, we should leverage that power and money like Jesus did—not to increase our standard of living, but to increase our standard of giving.*

felt "under obligation" to those who haven't heard about Christ (Rom. 1:14–17). God had revealed Himself to Paul in grace; how could Paul not yield his life for others? Are you leveraging your life for others as Jesus leveraged His for you?

3. The Holy Spirit must guide us as to which sacrifices *we*, personally, are to make.

In the more Baptist and Reformed-ish circles I run in, people are not exactly sure, practically speaking, what the Holy Spirit *does*, beyond regenerating our hearts and convicting us of sin.

I'm not going to attempt to answer the question of what all the Holy Spirit does here,[4] but I do believe the Holy Spirit actively guides us. In fact, in the area of generosity, I depend on it. How do I know which priorities of heaven I should leverage my limited resources for?

I don't hear a lot of audible voices and don't give that much weight to "holy hunches," but I do think that the Holy Spirit has to show us which of His mission priorities are for us. Without that guidance, I'm not sure what I would do. I'd feel like I was called to everything.

Now, again, this principle, if taken by itself, will lead you awry. In fact, if you only give because the Holy Spirit "tells you to," then your giving is not overflowing from a heart of gratitude. You are just following orders. Remember, God doesn't want people who give only because they are told. He wants people whose hearts rise up spontaneously and joyfully when they are given the chance to be generous.

4. God delights in our enjoyment of His material gifts.

I love to give my kids things they enjoy. God is certainly no different; Scripture tells us God is the ultimate Daddy (Luke 11:11–12). He loves to delight us with all kinds of blessings. Paul says in 1 Timothy 6:17, after reminding the rich of their responsibility to be generous, that it is "God, who gives us richly all things to enjoy" (NKJV). God gives us material blessings as gifts, and He is glorified when we enjoy them. Scripture makes this point in a number of places. For example,

- Psalm 104:15 says He gives food and wine (fruit juices for us Baptists) to *gladden our hearts*, not just to nourish our bodies. An Outback steak glorifies Jesus. Praise God.
- In John 2:1–11 it says that Jesus created really good wine at the wedding feast in Cana. He could have done the watered down, cheap and sufficient, "wartime" wine. (Again, for you fellow Baptists for whom this wine analogy is lost on, it would be like going to a wedding reception with Jesus where they run out of the little ham sandwiches, and Jesus makes a prime rib and shrimp buffet in their place.) The point is that Jesus provided good stuff for people at the party because He *loved* His Father's creation and knew that *by enjoying it* we glorify God.
- In Nehemiah 8, when the people were wondering how to express their gratitude for "rediscovering" the law, their first response was to weep. But Ezra and Nehemiah *corrected* the people, and said, instead, "Go

and enjoy choice food and sweet drinks, and send some to those who have nothing prepared. This day is sacred to our Lord. Do not grieve, for the joy of the Lord is your strength" (8:10 NIV). God wanted them to express their gratefulness in this case through a *lavish* party. Couldn't they have just gnawed on corn husks and vegetables and drank water and given the rest of their money to the poor? Of course. But at this moment God wanted them to party.

- When the woman anointed Jesus' feet in John 12, Judas objected because the price of the perfume poured out over Jesus' feet was $25,000, and that clearly could have bought a lot of food for the poor! But Jesus doesn't say, "You're right, Judas . . . Mary, come on, we're in a war . . . you should 'melt that stuff down' and use it for war-bullets." Rather, Jesus delighted in the extravagant, uncalled for, luxurious, over-the-top display of love. Now, you may object and say, "But anointing the feet of Jesus is different than spending $4 on a caramel macchiato for ourselves when we could drink water instead and give the money to missions." Of course you are right, but don't miss the point—*Jesus recognized other uses for money besides just evangelism and poverty relief.*[5]

Again, if you take this principle apart from the other five, you will get out of balance. "God has given me richly all things to enjoy" and "He doesn't need my money" can easily be used to justify an indulgent, self-serving lifestyle. But you can (and should!) recognize God's fatherly goodness to you in material blessings.[6]

You don't have to feel guilty about making lots of money. You don't have to feel guilty about enjoying some of the blessings of money. Paul said that not only did he know how to be abased; he also knew

> Scripture tells us God is the ultimate Daddy (Luke: 11:11–12). He loves to delight us with all kinds of blessings.

how to abound (Phil. 4:11–13 KJV). Some Christians seem to know how to be abased, but not how to abound. We must learn to receive both suffering and prosperity from God's hand. Larry Osborne says, "When God 'Abrahams' me (blesses me with prosperity), I'll give Him thanks, enjoy it, and share it generously; and when He 'Jobs' (the Old Testament prophet) me, then I'll thank Him, trust Him, and enjoy my relationship to Him. By God's grace, I know both how to be abased and how to abound. I can do all things through Christ who gives me strength."[7] I think this is precisely what Paul meant in that verse.

5. God, not money, should be our primary source of beauty and security.

Many of us save up money obsessively for a "rainy day"; others spend money frivolously to acquire the most up-to-date status symbols and creature comforts. For the former, money is their primary source of security; for the latter, their primary source of beauty.

To those who see money as their security, Jesus says, "Consider the birds of the air. They don't save money, yet God takes care of them" (Matt. 6:26, author paraphrase). God can take care of you better than money ever could. So don't worry about tomorrow, because God is better security than money.

To those who see money as their beauty, Jesus says, "Consider the flowers of the field. They don't spend a lot of money, yet God makes them beautiful . . . even Solomon in his glory days was not as pretty as the flowers!" (Matt. 6:28–29, author paraphrase).[8] In other words, God will add a beauty, significance, and enjoyment to your life that money cannot. So you don't have to spend all your money adding those things into your life. Let God be your beauty and security.

When we no longer see money as our primary source of security and beauty, we *naturally* will have more to give away.

> Christians who worship God, not money, need much less from the world to be happy and secure.

Christians who worship God, not money, need much less from the world to be happy and secure. They can, as we love to say around our church, live *sufficiently* and give *extravagantly*.

Furthermore, Jesus also told us that if we understood what was coming in the resurrection, we'd see heavenly treasures as much wiser investments than earthly ones. In the resurrection we will experience the blessings of creation at their fullest. So we don't have to get it all down here. What we miss out on down here, we'll experience the resurrection version of up there. So you never get to take a vacation to the Alps? Big deal. Do you know what the resurrected version of the Alps is going to look like? If Jesus' resurrected body was recognizable, could be touched, eat fish, but could also walk through walls, what is the rest of resurrected creation going to look like? You probably won't even have to fly coach up there to go see the Alps. You probably won't have to fly on an airplane at all. You'll probably fly yourself. So Jesus challenged us to think a little farther out and invest our resources in a way that reaps dividends for eternity (Matt. 6:19–22). As Randy Alcorn says, you can't take any of your money with you when you die, but you can send a lot of it on ahead of you.[9]

As God's Kingdom becomes our treasure, joyful generosity becomes our natural response.

6. Wealth-building can be wise.

God says it is OK, even biblically wise, to build wealth. Consider these clear instructions in Proverbs:

- "The crown of the wise is their wealth." (14:24)
- "Wealth gained hastily will dwindle, but whoever gathers little by little will increase it." (13:11)
- "Go to the ant, O sluggard; consider her ways . . . she prepares [and saves!] her bread in summer and gathers her food in harvest." (6:6–8)

Solomon goes so far in Proverbs 13:22 as to say that a wise man can leave an inheritance that blesses even his grandchildren! That's a pretty significant wad of cash that God expects some believers to die with.

In fact, building wealth can actually *increase* your ability to be generous. Having money on hand can allow you to be strategically generous when the right moment arises. Some of the earliest Christians had houses large enough to hold some of the first church meetings, which was good since they were kicked out of every other facility. The Good Samaritan was able to give his money to the man in need precisely because he had extra.

Furthermore, the most basic principle of economics is that money creates money. Through the compound interest that accumulates on sizable savings, you can give more away over a lifetime if you invest some of your money wisely than you could by simply ridding yourself of all of it as soon as you get it. Proverbs teaches that, and so does Jesus in the "parable of the talents" (see Matt. 25:14–30). Thus, sometimes the investment of a portion of your money is a more generous decision than giving it all away.

Now, again, if you held this principle alone (and not in tension with the others), it would lead to the hoarding of wealth, something Scripture clearly condemns (James 5:1–5). We must balance responsible saving with generous giving. People are dying *now*, and we must be generous to them now, not just at our death.

Clearly, however, the Bible indicates you can save money in a God-honoring way.

How Much Should Christians Give?

You've been in waiting for the bottom line. Fallen human nature loves laws, because we love self-justification. But laws keep us from dealing with the real issue—our heart. The law is easier to preach too—whether that's giving 10 percent; "giving away all the excess"; "living at the average American household salary and giving away everything above that"; using a PC instead of a Mac; drinking Folgers instead of Starbucks, etc. Laws preach nicely. But the gospel writers resist the temptation to reduce Christianity to laws. They focus on the heart.

That's why, I believe, the Bible gives us the matrix of these six principles and leaves them, in some ways, unresolved. These six principles will all be at work in a gospel-saturated heart. So, let's resist the temptation to add specificity where the Bible does not.

The bigger questions that we must ask about money are heart questions, like these:

What does your spending show that you delight in?

When you get an extra amount of money you weren't expecting, does your heart first go to what you want to buy for yourself, or the health and salvation this can provide for others? What does your spending show that you delight in?

Take a long hard look at your checkbook. What does that record of expenditures show that you love?

What does your saving show you find security in?

Who do you trust to take care of you in the future? Do you need to save *so much*? People are suffering *now*—and God has given you resources now to help them. Could we not save modestly and give away extravagantly? Cannot we depend on the God who provides for us today also to take care of us tomorrow?

Whose kingdom are you building?

The most fundamental question every disciple of Christ must ask himself is which kingdom is his *primary* pursuit.

> *The most fundamental question every disciple of Christ must ask himself is which kingdom is his primary pursuit.*

Quit thinking so much about the amount you're giving and think instead about the kingdom you're pursuing. Following Jesus means seeing your life as a seed to be planted for God's kingdom.

So, ask yourself: *What have you done with the majority of your resources up to this point in your life? How are you leveraging your talents now for God's kingdom? What have you spent the majority of your money on thus far? Where does the bulk of your treasure lie?*

Awakening from "the American Dream" to "the Gospel Reality"

American Christians have lived in a culture saturated by something we have learned to call "the American dream." The American dream is, in its essence, a good thing. It was the promise of freedom—the freedom to pursue life and prosperity without government or societal restraints.

I am very grateful to live in a country that has made it easy to become relatively wealthy. I've lived overseas under dictatorships and visited plenty of Communist countries. Believe me, I love the American dream.

> *As a disciple of Jesus, what matters most is what I do with the wealth that the American dream has afforded me.*

But as a disciple of Jesus, what matters most

is what I do with the wealth that the American dream has afforded me. Jesus did not put me here on earth to pursue self-benefit. He put me here to leverage my blessings, including the American dream, for the purposes of the gospel.

People who die without Christ go to hell forever. The only way they can hear about the gospel is through us. We are in a battle, and the casualties are real. We must awaken from the American dream to gospel reality.

We've only got one life to live, and a short time to live it. Thus, we should leverage our lives for all they are worth. And think about this, soberly: Soon

> Soon we stand before King Jesus, and we will give an account for what we did with what He placed in our hands.

we stand before King Jesus, and we will give an account for what we did with what He placed in our hands.

Do we dare take the resources provided to us by a Savior who bled and died for us and fill our lives with perks and privileges that simply make our lives more enjoyable?

I'd challenge you to pray the third part of The Gospel Prayer over your resources, and then follow where God leads you.

I'll warn you: praying this prayer with sincerity is danger-ous. It could radically alter your life. But Jesus, the gospel, and lost people all over the world are worth it.

"As You have been to me, so I will be to others."

CHAPTER 9

Urgent Mission

The gospel compels us to respond to others as Christ has responded to us. That's why we pray: *"As You have been to me, so I will be to others."*

We've seen how that first changes how we forgive others, and second how it compels us to yield our resources for their blessing. I want to talk now about how it pushes us out to the ends of the earth.

When I first surrendered to Jesus, I told Him I'd do whatever He asked me to do. All I needed was some instructions. I kept waiting for some kind of "Damascus Road" experience—where God knocked me out of my car and told me the plan, or at least spelled out in my Cheerios what He wanted from me. Something like, "J.D., take the gospel to Afghanistan." But nothing like that ever came. No bright lights. No voices. All my Cheerios ever spelled out was "*oooooooooooo.*"

So I chose a career path I thought I'd be good at and got on with it. But during my junior year of college, I was arrested by Romans 2:12, "For all who have sinned without the law will also perish without the law, and all who have sinned under the law will be judged by the law."

In Romans, Paul lays out a case why faith in Jesus is necessary for salvation, how people have to hear about Jesus in order to put faith in Him, and how we are the only ones they can hear it from. In Romans 2:12 Paul explains that even those people who haven't heard about God must answer to Him, because God has revealed Himself sufficiently to them through their consciences and the splendor of the creation. They may never have heard the name of Jesus, but they know there is a God, and they have rejected His authority and His glory. We all, religious and nonreligious alike, have rejected God. Because of that, we all stand condemned. Thus, Paul concludes, our only hope is an undeserved "second chance," and that comes by hearing the gospel.

It is hard to describe what happened that morning as I read that verse. It was as if that truth suddenly became real. I had understood it, before, propositionally, but for the first time in my life, I felt the weight of it. It was almost like when you are staring at one of those "magic eye" 3-D pictures that suddenly jumps out at you when you cross your eyes just right. The reality of whole nations of people perishing, having never heard about Jesus, gripped my soul.

You see, at most, one third of our world is Christian. That's if you count everyone who claims to be a Christian. That means *at least* 4.5 billion people are, by their own admission, non-Christian and therefore separated from God. The

Joshua Project, a Christian missions research organization, tells us that of that 4.5 billion, at least 2.25 billion have little to no access to the gospel.

2,250,000,000. *Individuals.*

It's easy to get lost in that statistic. Joseph Stalin once said, "The death of one is a tragedy. The death of a million is just a statistic." That's a chilling statement coming from a madman, but there's some truth in it. Statistics overwhelm. But when we are confronted with the death of an individual, we feel compassion, because we see in that person a reflection of ourselves. We identify with their pain.

These 2.25 billion are people created in the image of God, just like you and me. They have the same needs, wants, hurts, and desires you and I have. Each one is someone's son or daughter. Many are someone's mom or dad. They know what it is like to be lonely and afraid. Going to hell for them is every bit the tragedy that it would be for you or me.

As the weightiness of 2.25 billion *people* lost without God pressed in on my soul, I felt like I was suffocating. I just sat there, speechless.

> Going to hell for them is every bit the tragedy that it would be for you or me.

It didn't seem right to be going on about my life, pursuing my dreams, waiting on God to tell me what to do. We know what He wants us to do. Imagine you were walking by a railroad track and you came upon a young child lying on the tracks, hurt, and unable to move. You hear a train coming in the distance. If you pick the child up, you will rescue him; if you do not, he will die. What do you do? Do you get down on your knees, pray and ask God what His will is, and wait for a warm, fuzzy feeling confirming that it is His will that you rescue the child? Of course not. You know what God's will is. Save the child.

> People talk about "finding" God's will. It is not really "lost."

In relation to the unreached people groups of the world, we know what God's will is: "The Lord is not . . . willing that any should perish but that all should come to repentance" (2 Pet. 3:9 NKJV). People talk about "finding" God's will. It is not really "lost." His will is that lost people hear about Jesus and become saved.

That morning, confronted by that reality, I had three options:

1. *I could deny it.* I could deny the plain teaching in Romans that people are lost until they hear about Jesus and believe on Him. Picking and choosing what you want to believe from the Bible is called "liberalism." You conform the Bible to fit your personal preferences. But the Bible is not a buffet where you take what you want and leave what you don't. You and I don't judge the Bible; it should judge us. The path of liberalism is a dead end.

2. *I could ignore it.* I could put my head back in the sand and ignore the fact that billions of people around me were lost. I could go on about my life, letting Jesus take me to heaven and giving me fulfillment and meaning. But how could I do that now, knowing what I know? Ignoring truth doesn't change it.

Sadly, I believe, this is what the vast majority of the evangelical church is doing with their knowledge about heaven and hell. We go on about our lives as if hell were not real, or like there are not 2,250,000,000 people who have no chance of hearing the gospel except through us. We play while people perish.

3. *I could embrace it.* I knew this would be radical. It would lead to a dramatic reorientation of my life.

I chose number 3. That morning my prayer about what to do with my life changed from, *"God, if You spell out in my Cheerios for me to go, I'll go,"* to *"God, here am I. Please send me. Use my life, to the greatest extent possible, to bring salvation to others."*

I believe that is the prayer every disciple of Jesus should pray. Our prayer should not be "God, if You make a special appeal for me to do something about the lostness of the world, I'll do it." That's kind of a senseless prayer, because He has already told us what He wants for the world. Our prayer now should be that God guide us to our specific role. Whether we should be involved in the Great Commission is no longer the question. *How* we should be involved is the question.

God answered my prayer by allowing me to spend time overseas in one of the unreached people groups of the world, and now He's allowing me to pastor a church that sends out hundreds of students and young adults each year to take the name of Christ where He is not known.

Every disciple of Jesus should ask God to use his or her life maximally for His kingdom. Overseas missions will not be God's answer for everyone. But if we have really experienced the gospel, then we'll be asking God to use us in His mission. We will say something like this: "Lord, let my life be a seed for others, like Yours was for me, planted into the ground. Let my dreams die so that others might live. Show me how to best invest my life for You and not for me. *As You have been to me, I want to be to others.*"

Think about it: How could we not pray that? Where would *you* be without Jesus? According to Paul, you'd be at exactly the same place that a lot of people in the world are if you refuse to embrace the task (Rom. 10:14–17).[1]

> Where would you *be* without Jesus?

Martin Luther said that it wouldn't matter if Jesus had died a thousand times if no one ever heard about it. We are the only way they hear about it.

Now, let's remember here, lest we saddle ourselves with a burden we can't carry, that the work of salvation, from start to finish, is God's work. God didn't lay the Great Commission on our shoulders as if He expected us to go accomplish it for Him. Just as He is the only one who can save, He's the only One who empowers and supplies for the mission. Even after Paul laid out the case that people can only be saved if we preach to them, he says, "And how shall they preach, unless they are *sent*?" Notice, he doesn't say, "And how can they hear unless *we go*?" But, "How can they hear unless we *are sent*?" Paul still looks heavenward for the completing of the task. The Holy Spirit has to do the sending before the going does any good. The Holy Spirit anoints us, commissions us, and resources us. He'll use us and our stuff in the process, but don't confuse His doing it *through us* with Him telling us that we have to do it *for Him*. He gave us a promise, that *He* would build His church through us, not a charge that we were to build it for Him.[2]

That said, the breakdown in the system of sending, going, preaching, hearing, and believing isn't with any failure on God's part to "send." It's with our "going." When we present ourselves to God as willing goers, rest assured that He'll be a willing Sender.

That's what I did that morning in my dorm room: I presented myself to God and asked to be used by Him. I asked to be the seed put in the ground to die. For eighteen years now God has answered that prayer. That has included overseas assignments as well as some across the street.

When you pray the third part of The Gospel Prayer, *"As You have been to me, so I will be to others,"* be prepared for God to lead you to do something extraordinary. Be prepared for a radical reorientation of your entire life.

Our Freedoms versus the Gospel

We all have dreams about what we'd love to do with our lives. But are we willing to let our dreams die so that God can use us in His kingdom?

One of my favorite stories from Paul's life captures how Paul lived this way (Acts 16:16–34). Paul had been put in a Roman prison, not for something he did wrong but for something he did right. He had delivered a girl from demonic and economic exploitation. Rather than being rewarded, however, he was beaten, Roman-style, and then imprisoned. But as he lay there in chains that night, with open, bleeding wounds, he began to reflect on the goodness of God toward him and worshipped Him with a song.

In response, God sent an earthquake. The prison walls fell down, and Paul's chains fell off.

He was a free man.

And it was a God-given freedom too. After all, isn't God the one who sent the earthquake? Paul knew that God sometimes sent angels to free his messengers in prison; He had done that for Peter just a few chapters before (Acts 12). Wouldn't it have been reasonable to conclude that was what He was doing here too? Surely this was an answer to prayer!

Yet, as Paul prepared to walk into the open air, he saw in the distance a Roman soldier, with sword drawn, about to kill himself. The rule in those days was that if a Roman soldier lost a prisoner, for whatever reason, he had to pay with his own life. Paul was free, but he saw another man in chains.

Decision time. There stood Paul—with his God-given freedom on one hand, and his Roman captor on the other. What did Paul do? He turned his back on his freedom and walked back into the prison, joyfully and willfully, so he could share the gospel with his captor.

The Roman soldier, overwhelmed by this whole sequence of events, responded with a tremulous question, "Sirs, what must I do to be saved?" (Acts 16:30). I can't help but read in those words another question, "Why, Paul? What would make you do this? Why would you care about me?"

Paul would explain later, in a letter to the church at Philippi (which would have now included this Philippian jailor!) why he would do something like that. Paul explained that he himself had been in mortal danger when Jesus turned His back on His freedom in order to rescue him. Because Jesus entered into Paul's captivity, to save him, it only made sense, then, that Paul would do that same thing for others (Phil. 2:5–11).

We live in a world of captives, both physical and spiritual. We were once there ourselves.

Where would you be if Jesus chose to steward His resources as you are stewarding yours?

What are you doing with your life? How are you leveraging your resources, your free time, and your talents to see salvation come to others?

Have you evaluated your talents, your opportunities, and leveraged them for maximum kingdom impact? This is not just the duty of a select, specially-called-out few. Honestly, sometimes I think we invented this whole language of "calling" to mask the fact that most Christians are not really living as disciples of Jesus. Radical generosity and radical commitment to the mission is the response of every person who has experienced the grace of Jesus Christ. Following Jesus, being His disciple, means living as He lived. He leveraged His life for the lost.

Are you using your gifts, your time, and your opportunities to enrich yourself, or to bless the world with the knowledge of Jesus?

I can't tell you exactly what investing your life for God's kingdom will look like. God has put such a marvelous array of gifts and passions into His body that it looks different for each of His followers.

> *Sometimes I think we invented this whole language of "calling" to mask the fact that most Christians are not really living as disciples of Jesus.*

Maybe you can live on much, much less than you make, and give the rest away.

Maybe you could use your business skill overseas in a place where Christ is not well-known. Maybe you could create jobs for others there.

Maybe you could give your time to serve the poor in your community.

Maybe you could move into a poor neighborhood in your own city to be the presence of Christ there.

Maybe you could give your vacation time to go on mission trips around the world.

Over the last few years at our church I have seen people respond to the gospel in the most incredible ways. I've seen people resign from high-paying corporate jobs to come on our staff. I know of a husband, wife, and two teenage children who abandoned "the American dream" and went to live in a fundamentalist Muslim country. I've seen people give away investment properties so we could expand our ministries. I've seen people uproot from nicer neighborhoods to live in ghettos. I've seen a college student turn down a several-hundred-thousand-dollar job offer to go into church planting. I've seen students switch from majors with high earning potential to ones with low earning potential because they thought it would make them more useful for the Great Commission. I've seen others who took high-paying jobs and leveraged them for public witness. I've seen people get involved in our student and children's ministries. This past month we saw twenty-five people uproot from our church to go and plant a church in an unreached part of downtown Denver, Colorado. I've seen families open up their homes to refugees. We have a whole army of people in our church who have adopted children from around the world—not because they were unable to have one biologically, but because they wanted to do for someone what Jesus had done for them.

These people want to have something to lay at the feet of King Jesus when He comes again.

Does all of this sound radical to you? If so, *then you're getting it.* Jesus did not come to make slight alterations to our lifestyles. He called us to live for a completely different kingdom. To pick up His cross and live like He did.

> *Jesus did not come to make slight alterations to our lifestyles. He called us to live for a completely different kingdom.*

Stop waiting on God to tell you to offer your life for the kingdom. He's already done that. Instead, ask Him to show you *how best* to do it.

I pray that you'll embrace the lostness of the world and rearrange your life in light of it.

"But you are the only Christian I have ever known!"

For two years I served as a church planter in Southeast Asia. The last conversation I had there, almost ten years ago, left an indelible mark on my life.

An Islamic friend, whom I will call Ahmed, had come to say good-bye. He had been my best friend there. He befriended me at a very lonely time in my life and for two years, we talked, travelled, studied, and fished together.

I had tried a number of times to bring up Jesus to him, but Ahmed seemed eager to leave the subject alone. He was as committed a Muslim as I had ever met. He was kind of like an Islamic "youth pastor," volunteering his afternoons to serve underprivileged kids and teens. When I would talk about Jesus, he would smile and say, "You are a good man of faith. You were born in a Christian country and you honor the faith of your parents. I was born in a Muslim country and I honor the faith of mine. You were born a Christian and will die a Christian. I was born a Muslim and I will die a Muslim."

About a week before I left, I knew I had to have one more conversation with him. So, I sat him down and poured my heart out. I told him that, according to the Bible, only those who have believed on Jesus Christ for the forgiveness of their sins can enter God's kingdom. For fifteen minutes he sat politely and listened. He then thanked me for my friendship and left.

I did not see him again until the day I was preparing to return home. A few minutes before I was supposed to leave, he came to say good-bye. I could tell something was on his mind, so I asked him about it.

"Our conversation from a week ago," he said. "After we talked, I thought about how much I appreciated you for telling me so directly what you believed. But then I didn't think much of it . . . 'He is a Christian; I am a Muslim,' I thought, 'that is how each of us was born, and that is how it always will be.'

"But seven days after our conversation I had a dream.

"At first I thought it was one of those dreams that comes when I eat spicy fish. But I've had those kinds of dreams. This was different . . . In my 'dream,' I was standing on earth and suddenly, open before my feet was the 'straight and narrow way' leading to heaven.[3]

"And as I looked up along this pathway to heaven," he said, "*you* were on it! You arrived at heaven's gates, but the way inside was blocked by huge, brass doors. I thought to myself, 'That is where his journey ends. Who has the power to open those doors?' But then, as I watched, someone from inside knew you, and they called your name. The doors then swung open wide for you, and you went in . . . and then my heart broke because I really wanted to go with you. But then, the doors opened again and you came back out, walked back down the path a little ways, and stretched your hand out to me down here on earth. And you pulled me up to heaven with you. Do you think God is trying to tell me something?"

I would have no problem interpreting this one.

For the next hour I walked him through Romans and Acts, showing Him how Jesus, the God-man, had come to earth, lived as our substitute, died our death, rose again, and offered salvation to all who would believe.

> You are the only Christian that I know. Who will teach me the way of God?

What he said next is something I can never, ever forget. He said, "I *know* why Allah gave me that dream. He was telling me that you were sent here by God to show me the path that leads to heaven. You were to teach me God's ways and explain to me His *Injil* (gospel). But today, my friend, you are going home, and we will probably never see each other again. You are the only Christian that I know. Who will teach me the way of God?"

I would love to tell you that he became a believer. Sadly, he did not, and, to my knowledge, he has not.

We live in a world of Ahmeds. They are not a number. They are individuals.

Have you really thought what that means for us?

We cannot pretend it's not true. Someone asked Charles Spurgeon once if they thought people who had never heard about Jesus could be saved. His response went something like, "I don't believe they can be, but the better question is *"How could those of us who have known Jesus and failed to take Him to those who have not heard possibly be saved?"*

I heard a story several years ago about a man who was driving his car down an interstate outside of Los Angeles late one evening. A significant earthquake rumbled through the region and so the man pulled his car over on to the side of the road to wait it out. The earthquake was severe but over after a few seconds. So, the man pulled his car back onto the road, took a left onto a bridge, and began to crossover. About halfway across the bridge he noticed the taillights of the car in front of him disappear. He stopped his car, got out, and realized that a section of the bridge had fallen out during the earthquake. The car in front of him had driven into the chasm, at full speed, plunging nearly 75 feet into the water below.

The man turned around, and realized that several more cars were headed toward the break. He began to wave his arms frantically. People driving across a bridge outside of Los Angeles at 3 a.m. are not likely to stop for what looks like a crazy person on the side of the road, and so he watched as four cars drove past, plunging to their deaths below.

He then saw a large bus coming toward the break. He made up his mind that if that bus was going off the bridge, it had to take him with it. So he stood in the path and waved his arms. The bus honked its horn and flashed it lights, but the man would not move. The bus driver got out, saw the danger, and angled the bus so no more cars could go past.

What would you have done if you had been the one to discover the break in the bridge? You probably would have done just what that man did—passionately plead for people to stop.

People in the world who do not know Christ are headed for a destruction far worse than that presented by the fallen bridge. Millions more are headed there now.

Every day you should think about what Christ gave up so that you would not perish. Then, you should ask God to help you do for others what He has done for you.

Again, I'm warning you: this is a dangerous prayer. It will lead you to some radical changes. So I challenge you to pray it:

"As You have been to me, so I will be to others."

CHAPTER 10

Expect Great Things

When was the last time you prayed for something that actually happened? Maybe it's been a while. But think back to that moment, and let me ask you another question: When God moved, *were you surprised?*

So far in this gospel prayer we have considered (1) the freeness of God's acceptance of us, (2) the weightiness that should have with us, and (3) how it calls for a radical response of generosity toward others. In this final part of The Gospel Prayer, we'll see how the gospel moves us to audacious faith and great attempts on behalf of the Great Commission.

Here it is:

> *"As I pray, I'll measure Your compassion by the cross*
> *and Your power by the resurrection."*

Jesus gave a pretty remarkable promise to His disciples in John 15. He said that if we "remain in Him" (i.e., abide in His love), we could ask whatever we want and it would be given to us. If we lived with an awareness of His love *for others*, the kind of power in prayer we could tap into would blow our minds.

A few years ago I was doing a study of the major miracles in Scripture. In the midst of that study I noticed something I'd never seen before. Most of these miracles did not happen because someone was acting on a direct, spoken command from God. Most happened because somebody perceived what God probably wanted to do in a particular situation and asked Him to do it. The initiative for the miracle began with them.

A great example of that is the story of Shadrach, Meshach, and Abednego.

> *Most of these miracles did not happen because someone was acting on a direct, spoken command from God.*

In case you're unfamiliar with that story, here's a quick review of the plot: King Nebuchadnezzar is a short, balding, egotistical king who has brought together everyone in his global kingdom so they can bow down to a ninety-foot statue of himself, because he was still a little sensitive about the fact that people made fun of his strange name all throughout middle school. (Some license in interpretation has been taken.)

Shadrach, Meshach, and Abednego refuse because they know they can only bow down to the God of Israel. So, when the music starts, they don't bow. They stick out like a redneck at the opera.

Nebuchadnezzar calls them up in front of everyone to explain why they dared defy his authority. He is the world's most powerful ruler and has a fiery furnace to back it up.

Their reply has always intrigued me. They speak with a curious mixture of certainty and uncertainty about God's plan to deliver them:

> *"Our God whom we serve is able to deliver us from the burning fiery furnace, and he will deliver us out of your hand, O king." (Dan. 3:17)*

That sounds pretty certain that God is about to do something spectacular to show Nebuchadnezzer who is king.

But then they say,

> *"But if not . . ." (v. 18)*

What? Wait a minute, where'd the confidence go?

They are confident that God wants to show Nebuchadnezzar and the rest of the world that He is the only true God. Yet, they have no guarantee that God will do that by delivering them. He might do it by helping them suffer well in their pain. But they know He'll do something.

Why were they so sure God would use this opportunity to show off that He was the one, true God? Well, there's a little phrase at the beginning of Daniel 3 that should catch your attention. It says that Nebuchadnezzar had gathered

together people of every "tribe, tongue and nation." This was
the first time all the nations have been gathered together
since the scattering at the Tower of Babel. (Before the Tower
of Babel, everyone had spoken the same language; at Babel
God divided them up into languages and scattered them.)
And now they have been gathered by an egomaniac bent on
self-worship. God had said that He would gather the nations
around to worship Him.

Shadrach, Meschach, and Abednego knew there was no
way God would let Nebuchadnezzar steal His position. So
they asked God to show the nations that He was the only
One to be worshipped through them. And so it happened.
Nebuchadnezzar threw them into the fiery furnace, but
they walked out unscathed. Everyone knew that God, not
Nebuchadnezzar, was the world's true King.

Take a Dare on God

As indicated by their uncertain reply to Nebuchadnezzar,
Shadrach, Meshach, and Abednego had not been promised
that God would show up and vindicate them by deliverance.
They just took a dare on God. This pattern seems to be the
norm when God moves in the Bible.

Think about David approaching the field to fight Goliath.
Nowhere in 1 Samuel do we find God pulling David aside to
tell him how it's all going to go down: "OK, David. Here's
what's going to happen . . . You're going to hear this big oaf
Goliath talking smack, and you are to go out there with a
leather strap and five smooth stones . . . you paying attention,
David? I said five smooth stones. Then . . ." No, David simply

saw a situation where he knew what God wanted to do, and he took a dare on God to do it.

I'm using that language of "dare" intentionally. When the children of Israel had entered into the Promised Land, God had said to them: "Be strong and courageous . . ." (Josh 1:9). In English, "be strong" and "courageous" sounds redundant. In Hebrew, however, the two phrases are different. The verb for "be strong," indicates something like "be daring." God wanted them to be confident enough in Him to take a dare on Him.

> God wanted them to be confident enough in Him to take a dare on Him.

Caleb, a faith-filled octogenarian in the book of Joshua, does just that. He pointed at an unconquered mountain and rattled through his dentures, "I want to conquer that mountain for God." And then he hobbled up the mountain with his walker, kicking giant-tail and taking names (Josh. 14:11–12).

A few years earlier, Joshua had found himself in a battle in which he thought he needed a little more daylight to finish the job. So, he asked God to make the sun stand still (Josh. 10:1–14). Nowhere in the Bible had God promised He would make the sun stand still if Joshua needed longer days. But Joshua asked anyway. And God did it.

Not only did God "stop the sun" for Joshua, He raised him one by throwing down "large stones from heaven on them as far as Azekah, and . . . there were more who died because of the hailstones than the sons of Israel killed with the sword"

(10:11). The point: God loves to fight for His people when His people understand what His will is and "take a dare" on Him to do it!

If anything, we see this principle intensified in the life of Jesus.

A woman once snuck up behind Jesus to touch the hem of His garment. For twelve years she had been defiled by an "issue of blood," a menstrual flow that made her perpetually unclean. She'd spent all her money on physicians, but no one could help her. Hearing about Jesus, she thought, *I bet He can do something . . . He has so much power that just brushing His clothing might heal me.*

> God loves to fight for His people when His people understand what His will is and "take a dare" on Him to do it!

When everyone discovers what she's done, they expect Jesus to be angry. Jesus' response to her, however, is anything but anger. He says, "Daughter, your faith has made you well" (Luke 8:48). She believed in Jesus' compassion, and that's what she found.

Probably my favorite part of this story is that Jesus' initially responded to her as if He didn't even have control of the healing power that went out of His body. He says, "Someone touched me, for I perceive that power has gone out from me . . ." (Luke 8:46). It is almost like healing jumped from His body as a reflex. The point? God's help flows out reflexively to those who presume upon His grace and power.

In another story recorded in Mark 7, a Gentile woman, despised by most Jews, asked Jesus to cast a demon out of her daughter. Jesus' response to her has to be the most politically-incorrect statement in all the New Testament: "It is not right to take the children's bread and throw it to the dogs" (Mark 7:27).

Dog? That's doesn't seem very nice. Some scholars try to soften what Jesus said by saying dog here means something more like "little puppy." Maybe so, but He's still referring to her as a dog. And calling someone a "dog" in that day was even worse than it would be in ours, because dogs were unclean!

The woman is unphased. She recognizes that Jesus' statement is not a racial slur, but a description of her unworthiness. She doesn't dispute her unworthiness for Jesus' attention; instead, she says, "Yes, Lord, yet even the little dogs under the table eat from the children's crumbs" (v. 28 NKJV). In other words, "Jesus, there is so much grace and power on Your table, that there is an abundant supply even for a dog like me."

Wow. She put all her hope in the compassion and power of Jesus. And she found it was a never-ending supply.

> The person who received the miracle was not responding to a "direct order" from God. They simply perceived the compassion and power of God, and then asked God to act on it. And God answered.

Don't miss the point. In all of these situations, the person who received the miracle was not responding to a "direct order" from God. They simply perceived the compassion and power of God, and then asked God to act on it. And God answered.

Let me show you one more biblical example of this kind of holy presumption. This account is one of the most important miracles in the New Testament, I believe, for how we see ministry.

A Ministry-Defining Miracle

Jesus had taught all day and the 5,000+ people in His audience was hungry. So Jesus turned to His disciples and asked them what *they* thought He should do. This was really just "a test," the apostle John wrote, "For He Himself knew what He would do" (John 6:6 NKJV).

A test. So what exactly was He "testing"? He wanted to see whether or not His disciples understood how willing and able He was to feed that multitude.

The disciples failed this test miserably, of course. One disciple told Jesus to send them away. Another got kind of testy and said something like, "Yeah, Jesus, great idea . . . we could all go get jobs and work for eight months and then pool our money and we might be able to buy them each a slice of salami and a Cheez-It." Jesus, however, patiently took the five small loaves of bread and two fish of a young boy's lunch (a Hebrew Happy Meal) and multiplied it so that there were twelve baskets full of leftovers, one for each of the disciples to take home as a memento of their unbelief.

Jesus showed them that day that there was no shortage in His ability or willingness to feed the multitude. *Why was He teaching them that?* Because for the rest of their lives they were going to be standing in front of spiritually starving multitudes, in need of the gospel, and they needed to know just how willing and able He would be to feed those multitudes with the Bread of Life.

Jesus has not changed. He is still willing and able to feed the multitudes. What He wants us to do is lay hold of His willingness, in prayer, and release His power into a world in desperate need.

Intercessory Faith

We teach a concept at our church called "intercessory faith." Intercessory faith means believing in Jesus' willingness on behalf of someone else. Many times we see that word "intercession" and we think "prayer." Intercession is prayer, of course, but people sometimes think that in prayer we act like God's CNN news-ticker reel and tell God a bunch of stuff He wouldn't otherwise know. After we pray, God says, "Oh . . . I had no idea that was going on. Thanks for telling Me. Now I can go down and fix that."

Intercessory prayer is not informing God on behalf of someone else; it is believing God on behalf of somebody else.

Shortly after I left Southeast Asia, the island on which I lived was ravaged by a tsunami that took the lives of nearly 200,000 people. I returned there a few months later

> *Intercessory prayer is not informing God on behalf of someone else; but believing God on behalf of somebody else.*

and stood on the beach, angry at God. *Why, God? Why? You could have spoken a word and sent a wave of salvation. Instead You sent a wave of destruction.*

God spoke to me on that beach. Not audibly—but clearly. He said, "I want to send a wave of salvation, and I will. That's why I want you here. Believe in My goodness and My power, and thereby release a wave of My compassion onto this island. God places His people in situations where He wants them to believe in His goodness and power, thereby releasing it into the situation."

Our most important work is believing.[1] Belief unlocks the power for the mission of God. We are to believe in God's tenderness and generosity for lost people, *and ask accordingly.*

No Shortage

There is no shortage in God's willingness or ability to save. The shortage is in our unbelief that He is as compassionate and powerful as the gospel says He is.

> We are to believe in God's tenderness and generosity for lost people.

Do you *really* believe that God is as compassionate and powerful as the gospel reveals Him to be? Does the size of your prayers reflect that belief?

Recently I was praying for my children, particularly burdened by some challenges they were facing. In the midst of praying I was filled with this overwhelming sense of *God's love* for them. It was a pretty amazing thought: God loves my children even more than I do.

In Luke 11:11, Jesus said this: "What father among you, if his son asks for a fish, will instead of a fish give him a serpent?" Any of you parents ever do that? Your kid asks you for a sandwich and you slip him a live cobra? Of course not. Yet, Jesus says, "If you then, who are evil, know how to give good gifts to your children, how much more will the heavenly Father give . . ." (v. 13). *Evil* is a pretty strong word to use to describe our relationship to our children. Most of us love our children. But compared to God's love for them, our love seems "evil." God loves my children, and whomever I am praying for, more than I can possibly comprehend.

Do you pray with a sense of God's great love for those for whom you were praying?

What would your prayers look like if you believed that the cross really was the measure of God's compassion for someone?

When Charles Spurgeon would pray for sick people in his congregation, he felt that tenderness. He would often tear up, biographers say, and say something like, "God, I cannot bear to see my children suffer. How can You bear to see Yours? If I could help them, I would. Won't You show compassion here to Your child?"

Charles Spurgeon was no silly "name it and claim it" theologian. He recognized that sometimes God says "no" to our prayers, because sometimes God has a better plan than physical healing at the moment. But that didn't keep him from sensing the tenderness of God for people as he prayed. Spurgeon held up God's goodness before God and released God's power into a situation.

In the next chapter, I'll explain a little more fully how you deal with unanswered prayer, but suffice it here to say that our confidence in the compassion and power of God should not be affected when He doesn't answer our prayers like we think He should. The cross is the measure of His compassion, and the resurrection the measure of His power. When we can't understand what God is doing in our circumstances, we can hold on to what we see revealed about Him in the cross. We can still know that God is *good*. He cares about us, feels our pain, and even weeps when we weep (John 11:35). He is a better father to His children than we are to ours. We should embrace that as we pray.

> *What would your prayers look like if you believed that the cross really was the measure of God's compassion for someone?*

So, Ask!

There seems to be no limit to what God will do when we perceive His willingness to help and ask Him to do it. As Jesus said in John 15:7, if we perceive His love for others, and understand that He came to seek and save the lost, and that He wants to bring salvation to sinners for the glory of the Father, then we can ask "whatever [we] wish," and He'll give it to us.

There is no shortage of compassion in God. The shortage is in our willingness to believe in that compassion.

The tragedy of wasted opportunity

Here is a weighty thought to consider as I close this chapter: If God really is as willing and able to save as the gospel indicates He is, and a key reason He doesn't pour out that power is because you and I never ask Him to, doesn't that make us responsible, in part for, the blood of millions who might have been saved, but weren't, because we never asked?[2]

I know that the Bible teaches that God is sovereign and God will save all He has determined to, and not one will be lost (John 6:37, 39). But the Bible also teaches us that He has placed His power at our disposal, to be released by faith. He will hold us accountable if we fail to access it.

Hudson Taylor, the great missionary to China, felt this *intensely*:

> We have to do with One who is Lord of all power and might, whose arm is not shortened that it cannot save, nor His ear heavy that it cannot hear; with One whose unchanging Word directs us to ask and receive that our joy may be full, to open our mouths wide, that He may fill them. And we do well to remember that this gracious God, who has condescended to place His almighty power at the command of believing prayer looks not lightly on the bloodguiltiness of those who neglect to avail themselves of it for the benefit of the perishing. . . .
>
> In the study of that divine Word, I learned that to obtain successful workers, not elaborate appeals for help, but first earnest prayer to God to thrust forth

laborers. . . . I had no doubt but that if I prayed for fellow-workers, in the name of the Lord Jesus Christ, they would be given. I had no doubt but that, in answer to such prayer, the means for our going forth would be provided, and that doors would be opened before us in unreached parts of the Empire. . . . The sense of bloodguiltiness became more and more intense. Simply because I refused to ask for them, the laborers did not come forward, did not go out to China: and every day tens of thousands in that land were passing into Christless graves![3]

The gospel reveals to us how willing God is to save. We should ask accordingly.

So where has God placed you, and on whose behalf are you supposed to believe? Do you realize how much power is available, if we would only believe?

Matthew 13:58 is one of the saddest verses in the New Testament. It says that Jesus did not do many mighty works in Nazareth "because of their unbelief." It was not that Jesus was unwilling or unable to work there, it was that there was no one to believe Him and thereby release His power. I never want that to be said of my city, my church, or my family.

I am confident this book has found its way into the hands of someone whose school or city God wants to turn upside down. Or maybe God is stirring your heart to go to one of the 6,600 unreached people groups. Maybe you will believe in God's compassion for that group, and through your faith their salvation will become reality. Maybe you are the first believer in your family, and God will use your faith to bring the rest of your family to Him. Wherever you are, expect great things from God, and then attempt great things for Him.[4]

Pray with the confidence that comes from the gospel:

"As I pray, I'll measure Your compassion by the cross and Your power by the resurrection."

CHAPTER 11

"But if Not . . ."

Shadrach, Meshach, and Abdnego came out of the furnace with even their eyebrows intact. Joshua had an extended period of daylight. The woman with the issue of blood was healed. These things give us confidence in God's willingness to help us, and therefore we can boldly pray:

> *"As I pray, I'll measure Your compassion by the cross and Your power by the resurrection."*

But here's the obvious question: What if He says no? For every deliverance from a fiery furnace, there are ten martyrs who die in its flames. So what do you do when the ministry flops? Or your friend rejects the gospel? Or your teenage son turns away from the faith? Or God doesn't heal you?

I've had situations where I couldn't see why God would not give me what I was asking for. My requests seemed to be in line with His purposes. So why didn't He answer?

"But if not . . ."

Those are the haunting words that Shadrach, Meschach, and Abednego used to conclude their speech to King Nebuchadnezzar. They knew that God's plan might not include their deliverance, at least in the here and now.

Just because God doesn't answer your prayer the way you think He should doesn't mean that He is any less compassionate or any less in control. It doesn't even mean you missed the will of God in what you were asking for.

John the Baptist was a Spirit-filled man with a Spirit-fueled ministry, but his ministry ended in (seeming) failure. His popularity vanished. No more soldiers were being baptized in repentance and Jewish leaders no longer cowering before His prophetic voice. He "dreamed great things for God," and he was beheaded.

Faith-filled prayers and Spirit-filled ministry do not always produce large, impressive movements.

The church I pastor is now a fairly large one, and we are seeing some truly God-sized things happen in our midst. Prior to this, however, I led a college ministry (at this same church) that I had been sure God was going to use to send thousands to the mission field. There were about 120,000 college students within a fifty-mile radius of the church, and I asked God to start a world-changing movement among them. At the end of two years of faith-filled labor, I had about twenty students in my ministry, most of whom were not very committed to the church. Needless to say, it wasn't quite the Acts 2 experience I had been hoping for.

Before that I spent two years preaching Christ in a foreign country, expecting He would turn the nation upside down for His glory. I only saw two people come to Christ.

There are times when you ask God for something and He doesn't give it to you. So what does that mean? That God is not as favorably disposed to you as you had thought?

The questions about why God allows tragedy, evil, and suffering are worth a book unto itself.[1] But how God feels about us, and how He relates to us, has been forever established in the gospel. What I want to help you see in this chapter is how you respond when God doesn't act like you think He should.

How to Respond When God Doesn't Act

What do you do when you are asking for great things according to God's compassion and you don't seem to be getting an answer?

1. Keep asking

Jesus taught His disciples that there were some things God would only give in response to persistent prayer. To illustrate this, He told a story about a crabby old dishonest judge who granted a poor widow her request simply because she annoyed him to death about it (Luke 18:1–6). He then told us that prayer sometimes worked like that.

I'm sure glad that Jesus made this analogy, not me. Comparing God to a capricious, unjust ruler? Jesus' point was not to compare the Father to an unjust judge, but to *contrast* Him with one. If even an unjust judge would grant a petition to a woman simply because she refused to let it go, then surely God will pay attention to the persistent requests of the children that He loves. Luke says that He told His disciples this story because He wanted them to not give up praying.

Many of the greatest victories in the kingdom of God came after it looked like the door had been permanently closed. For example, the door looked "closed" for getting the children of Israel out of Egypt. They had been in slavery for more than four hundred years and their situation was getting worse, not better. The door looked "closed" for Elijah to demonstrate to Ahab and the children of Israel that Jehovah was the true God, but Elijah went ahead and built his altar anyway. The door looked "closed" for Paul to get to Rome. But each of these great men of God kept asking and kept believing. Had they given up praying in the tenth hour they would have forfeited the victory God intended to give to them in the eleventh. The early church prayed all night to get Peter out of prison—evidently one casual mention at a prayer meeting evidently was not enough.

You may not have gotten your answer yet, so keep asking. The whole analogy of knocking Jesus uses for prayer in Luke 11:9 reinforces this idea: you don't rap the door once and wait. Knocking means to hit repeatedly. Praying means asking repeatedly.

Paul gives us a glimpse into his persistence in prayer in 1 Corinthians 16:9, "A great and effective door has opened to me, *and* there are many adversaries" (NKJV). Not "a great door seemed open to me, *but* there were many adversaries so I concluded it was closed," but "God opened a great door *and* there were many adversaries." Paul saw the presence of adversaries, obstacles, and closed doors as opportunities to keep pressing, not signals to give up. In fact, Paul had to be told to *quit* asking for something in 2 Corinthians 12:9. God finally sent down a message and said, "Paul, let this one go. You're not going to get it. You're going to get extra grace instead."

> *Paul saw the presence of adversaries, obstacles, and closed doors as opportunities to keep asking and keep pressing, not signals to give up.*

I'll be honest with you: this one is a mystery to me. If it is God's will to give us something, why not give it the *first* time we ask for it? What is clear is that God does some things only in response to persistent, unrelenting request. So keep asking.

2. Understand that God often accomplishes His good plan through our "unanswered" prayers

God will achieve all of His good ends. But He sometimes chooses ways that are mysterious to us.

Hebrews 11 describes two groups of believers who received two completely different kinds of answers to their prayers:

> *God does some things only in response to persistent, unrelenting request.*

. . . [some] through faith conquered kingdoms, enforced justice, obtained promises, stopped the mouths of lions, quenched the power of fire, escaped the edge of the sword, were made strong out of weakness, became mighty in war, put foreign armies to flight. Women received back their dead by resurrection. (vv. 33–35)

But there were also believers who:

. . . were tortured, refusing to accept release. . . . Others suffered mocking and flogging, and even chains and imprisonment. They were stoned, they were sawn in two, they were killed with the sword. They went about in skins of sheep and goats, destitute, afflicted, mistreated. (vv. 35–37)

Those are two very different groups. But the writer of Hebrews points to both of them as examples of faith and shows how God used both to complete His work on earth: "All these, though commended through their faith, did not receive what was promised" (v. 39).

I know what you are saying: "Please, Lord, let me be in group #1." Me too. But God has a purpose for both. Both are part of His plan. In one group, God showed off His *power* by giving them what they asked. In the other, He showed off His *value* by letting them testify that He was better than life.

At the end of the day, God's power is not primarily about victory over your particular situation. It's about the glory of His name on earth. Sometimes He does that by giving you victory over an obstacle; other times He does that by letting you suffer to show a watching world that He is better than anything else on the earth.

This has profound implications for one particular stream of religious thought right now. The so-called "prosperity gospel" teaches that it is never God's will for His people to be poor or sick or troubled in any way. Proponents of such beliefs call on people to see the evidence of God's blessing as material and physical well-being.

Let me be blunt: The prosperity gospel is a lie. God does love to give gifts to His children, and He delights in our successes. But the greatest prosperity is not driving a new car; it is knowing Him and having a life that brings glory

> *Preaching a message that says if you come to Jesus, He will make you rich is not only wrong, it leads people to idolatry rather than faith.*

to Him. Preaching a message that says if you come to Jesus, He will make you rich is not only wrong, it leads people to idolatry rather than faith. It leads people to use Jesus, not love Him.

God is glorified when sick people get well, but He's also glorified when sick people die well. We see this in the story of Shadrach, Meshach, and Abednego. When they had come safely through the furnace, Nebuchadnezzar said:

> *"Blessed be the God of Shadrach, Meshach, and Abednego, who has sent his angel and delivered his servants, who trusted in him, and set aside the king's command, and yielded up their bodies rather than serve and worship any god except their own God." (Dan. 3:28)*

Nebuchadnezzar gave glory to God not only because God delivered Shadrach, Meshach, and Abednego, but because they showed that God was more valuable to them than even life. Nebuchadnezzar would never have been able to see that had Shadrach, Meshach, and Abednego not gone through the fire. Suffering puts in stark relief the value of God above all things.

> We don't measure God's compassion by whether He answers our request like we think He should. We measure God's compassion by the gospel.

When our circumstances make us ask where God is, we anchor our souls in the God who gave Himself for us at the cross.

That leads to principle number 3.

3. Never stop believing

It is easy to believe in the love and power of God when you are seeing it manifested in your circumstances. Believing in God's love is harder, however, when He's not answering a prayer the way you think He should.

For years, atheists have advanced an argument against God based on the presence of evil in the world. It goes something like this: *If there were a God who is infinite in love, He would want to stop pain. If He is infinite in power, He could stop pain. Therefore, since pain exists, God must not.*

Perhaps you've asked a similar question, even as a believer:

- God, why won't You bless my ministry?
- God, why aren't I married yet?

- God, why isn't my business prospering? I'd use the profits to bless others!
- God, why won't You heal me?
- God, don't You see? Why won't You help? Don't You care? Do You not love me?

I can't answer all the "why" questions, but I do know this: We must not reinterpret how God feels about us based on our circumstances. The cross settles forever how God feels about us, and the resurrection shows us how much power He is using to bring about His good plan for our lives.

The cross also points us to the mysteries of how God works. If there were ever a time when it looked like God was absent and evil was in control, it was when Jesus, the supposed beloved Son of God, was being tortured to death. We know now that there was never a time when God was *more* in the driver's seat. He was accomplishing our salvation in that moment. Something that appeared to be a great victory for evil turned out to be the best part of His plan. He didn't bring salvation despite the cross, but actually *through* it. That means He is working His greatest plans out even in your worst moments too.

> *We must not reinterpret how God feels about us based on our circumstances.*

It shouldn't be surprising that sometimes God's greatest works are beyond our comprehension right now. If God's wisdom is as high above mine as His power is above mine, does it not make sense that some of the ways He works out His love on earth might be beyond my comprehension right now?

Think about how much greater God's power is than yours. He made the galaxies with a word; you can't figure out how to get the clock on your DVD player to quit flashing "12:00." If that is comparable at all to how much greater His wisdom is than ours, does it not make sense to you that some of what He does may not make sense to you at the moment?

Because of what we learn about God from the gospel, we can trust that sometimes He is bringing His love to bear in our lives even when He doesn't answer our prayers the way we want Him to. He is our Father, and because fathers know more than children they sometimes say no to a child's request.

In the previous chapter, we saw how Jesus taught us to look at God like a loving Father. He asked us, in Luke 11, to consider what we would do if our son asked us for a piece of fish to eat. Would we give him a cobra instead? Well, how about: if your kid asks you for a cobra, would you give *that* to him? I hope not. You'd tell him no *because* you love him.

God is a better and wiser father to us than we are to our children. Sometimes He says no *because* He loves us and has a greater plan than we can comprehend at the moment. Much of the reasoning behind the "no's" I give my kids they can't understand yet. My four-year-old says, "But Dad, why can't I put this fork in those little holes in the wall? It looks like it fits." "Alternating currents" are still a little beyond her, so I just say, "For now, child, trust me. Don't put the fork in the socket."

Which is greater? The gap between my four-year-old's understanding of reality and mine; or, *mine and God's?*

So it makes sense to me that some of what He does doesn't make sense to me. Yet sometimes God's negative answers to my prayers are the most loving thing He could do for me. I've heard it said this way: "God sometimes answers our prayers by giving us what we would have asked for had we known what He knows."

> God sometimes answers our prayers by giving us what we would have asked for had we known what He knows.

The bottom line is this: We should never give up praying for God's power to break into our lives, but at the end of the day we rest on the love of God demonstrated at the cross, even if we can't see how it is being manifested at the moment in our circumstances.

4. Abide in Jesus

Unanswered prayer often provides you the opportunity to consider whether or not Jesus really is enough for you. As we've learned, "abiding in Jesus" means, literally, "making our home in His love for us," to find hope in the good plan He is working through us, even in our pain. To find satisfaction in His presence with us, even when we have nothing else.

> We should never give up praying for God's power to break into our lives.

This morning I had breakfast with a friend with whom I had gone to seminary. Three years ago he was diagnosed with leukemia. Every ministry dream he had was taken away. He told me that as he lay on his back in a hospital room, he was forced to ask himself if Jesus really was enough for him. If he never has kids and none of his ministry dreams come true, is Jesus enough to have joy now?

Sometimes God strips you of success so that you can see what you really abide in. Sometimes He wants you to have nothing but Him so you can know that He really is enough. As Larry Crabb says, "You might never really know Jesus is all that you need until He is all that you have."

> Sometimes He wants you to have nothing but Him so you can know that He really is enough.

The extent to which you abide in Jesus is measured by your ability to be joyful in all circumstances. If your joy varies based on your succession, your job, or your relationships status, that means you aren't really abiding in Him—you're abiding in those things. Whatever controls your joy is what you abide in.

When God is not answering your prayers the way you'd like Him to, you need to press into the gospel. You need to anchor your soul in the compassion demonstrated at the cross and the power demonstrated at the resurrection.

You need daily to remind yourself:

⤜⤚

"As I pray, I'll measure Your compassion by the cross and Your power by the resurrection."

PART 3

Toward a Gospel-Centered
Understanding of Life

CHAPTER 12

Why Are There "Commands" in Scripture?

As you pray through The Gospel Prayer, day in and day out, I believe the same thing will happen to you that has happened to me: Your heart will burst alive with spiritual fruits. Your life will be transformed as you continually marvel at what God has done for you in Christ. Your passion for God will grow greater than your attractions to sin. You will begin to mirror, instinctively, that same grace, love, and mercy shown you in the gospel.

That's what being "gospel-centered" is really all about—not moving past the gospel, but continually going deeper into it. It's about realizing that the gospel is the final answer to every issue and problem in life and about seeing the whole world through the lens of the cross.

As we have explored how the gospel changes us, there are certain issues I've left on the table until now. These are good, valid questions you probably have had as you considered just how deeply the gospel can change you when you center yourself on it.

The first question is a very practical one, and one that arises just from reading the Bible: If the gospel changes internally, on the spot, so that we desire what is right, why are there so many "commands" still in the New Testament? Doesn't the whole concept of "commands" imply that we need to be told to do something that we otherwise might not do? If right behavior came naturally, why would we need to be commanded to do?

> *If God has really changed us with the gospel, why do we still need to be commanded to do anything?*

You can't escape the fact that there are commands on virtually every page in the New Testament. They range from instructions on how to treat your employer to how to raise your children to who it's OK to sleep with. But if the gospel gives us the heart that fulfills the law, why does God still provide us with these rules and instructions? Are they just training wheels for Junior Varsity Christians?

As our church has rediscovered the idea of gospel-centeredness, this question has surfaced a number of times. Once, after a series of sermons in which I laid out a vision for where we as a church were going and what we needed each member to be doing to get there, I received a scathing letter telling me that during that sermon I had abandoned the gospel and fallen back into legalistic manipulation to coerce people into doing what I wanted them to do! If I just preached the gospel people would naturally do what they were supposed to do and I wouldn't have to urge them to do anything, they said. In telling the church that we each had a responsibility to give, to serve, and bless our community, I had abandoned the gospel.

Is that true? Does the spirit of commands violate the principle gospel-centered change?

Not at all. Here are three reasons the New Testament still gives us commands:

1. *The commandments enlighten our darkened hearts.* The apostle Paul explains in Romans 1 that the problem of the fallen human heart is twofold. First, he says, our foolish hearts are darkened, making us *ignorant of much of what is right.* He goes on to say that our sinful hearts are also perverse, often *hating the right even when we know what it is.*

God's salvation of us includes teaching us what is right (by giving us instruction and commands) and remaking our hearts so that we love what is right (through the power of the gospel). Both commandment and gospel have a role.

The laws of God are like railroad tracks, pointing us in the direction to go. Trains need tracks to run on. But those tracks do nothing to power the engine.[1] Similarly, laws, in themselves, are unable to give us the power to do them. The gospel is the power of God for salvation. Jerry Bridges sums it up well,

> God's love provides us with the motivation for obedience, while God's laws provide the direction for the biblical expressions of love.[2]

2. *Obedience to the commandments limits the damage of our sin. When* we sin, we hurt God, others, and ourselves. *Sin* begins as a perverse desire, which is destructive enough in and of itself, but as we act on it, the destruction spreads. I am to obey the commandments even when I don't want to if for no other reason than I don't want to spread the destructive power of my sin.

James compares sin's destructiveness to the gestation process, "Then [sinful] desire when it has conceived gives birth to sin, and sin when it is fully grown brings forth death" (James 1:15). The first thing a doctor usually does is try to limit the damage of a disease. We obey the commandments even when we don't feel like it because we don't want to see our sinful desires bring forth death in our lives or the lives of others.

For example, if I am tempted to adultery, I must say no to it, even if in a particular moment I truly desire it. Why? Because I know that indulging in adulterous lusts takes my blaspheming of God's name a step further, and has devastating consequences for my family, my church, the woman I slept with, and me.

I don't just say, "Well, adultery is what is in my heart, and I can't correct my heart through externally-focused religious rules. So I might as well act on it and hope later God changes me." I say a profound "no" to the temptation because of all the destruction it brings.

I don't satisfy myself by simply having resisted the urge, however, I bemoan the state of my heart that desires impurity.

Just because I resisted the temptation to adultery does not mean I have nothing of which to repent. I must confess the twisted distortion of my heart and ask God to make it new.

And I must dwell on the God of purity who died on a cross for my impurity, because that will move me to hate impurity like He does.

3. *Disciplining ourselves to practice certain behaviors helps us develop a love for them.* Obedience to the commandments gives us a chance to develop a love for the One whose character they reflect. That may be a little hard to grasp, so let me explain.

James K. A. Smith makes the case in *Desiring the Kingdom* that the way we learn to love certain things is by participating in habits and practices that train us to love them. If our daily routines are tuned to indulge the lusts of the flesh, for example, we will grow in our love for those things. If our habits put us face-to-face with the beauties of the gospel, however, we will grow to love those instead.[3]

Appetites, you see, *grow* as you use them. Have you ever gone out to eat at your favorite steakhouse and gorged so much that when you're done you say, "Ugggh. I don't think I'll ever eat again!"? Four hours later, however, you are scrounging around in the pantry for a Pop-Tart. And the next time you go to the steakhouse, you eat even more. The appetite for food grows as you feed it.

This is true with all of our appetites. People who struggle with pornography often say that the more they fed their appetite for illicit sex, the stronger and darker that appetite became. The lazier you are, the stronger becomes your desire to sit around on the couch and do nothing. The more we get into God's Word, pray, and practice purity, the more we desire those things. Thus, disciplining ourselves to do what we don't always want to do helps us learn to love the things we should love.

Of course, simply practicing those things is not enough in and of themselves. Spiritual disciplines must be accompanied by a deep saturation in the gospel. The gospel changes the desires and cravings of the heart. The whole purpose of the disciplines, in fact, is to give you opportunity to think about, and meditate on, and move within the gospel. Spiritual disciplines are like wires that connect us to the power of the gospel. They have no power in themselves, but they connect us to the place from which the power flows. They are gateways to the gospel, but not the gospel itself.

> Disciplining ourselves to do what we don't always want to do helps us learn to love the things we should love.

Say you don't "feel" like reading the Bible; instead you "feel" like watching TV. Is "making yourself" read the Bible simply legalism? No. By feeding your soul the Word of God, you are training your heart to love it. As you read the Word of God, and encounter the God within it, your love for Him and His Word will grow. If you choose, however, to watch TV, your appetite for laziness and the lusts of the flesh are likely to grow instead.

> Spiritual disciplines are like wires that connect us to the power of the gospel.

Thus, the next day you will desire more TV and less of God, and if you indulge the flesh again, on and on it will go in a downward cycle. As you feed the flesh, your appetite for the flesh grows. As you feed the Spirit, your appetite for Him grows. This is the point Paul makes after one of the greatest explanations of gospel-centered change in the Bible: "Do not be deceived, God is not mocked; for whatever a man sows, that he will also reap. For he who sows to his flesh will of the flesh reap corruption, but he who sows to the Spirit will of the Spirit reap everlasting life" (Gal. 6:7–8 NKJV).

When my kids lie, I don't simply say, "Well, you lied because that's what was in your heart at the moment. I'm not going to force you to tell the truth, because I don't want to create little Pharisees. Just meditate on the gospel and hopefully you'll quit desiring dishonesty." Instead, I "coerce" them to tell the truth (by giving punishments for telling lies). My hope is that in practicing truth they will learn to love it, because when we act in accordance with God's design we experience a measure of fulfillment that comes from acting in harmony with how we were created.

I recognize, however, that my commands to tell the truth can only take them so far. So in as much as I am "making" them tell the truth, I am also teaching them about the beauty of the God of truth, who kept His promises to us even when it cost Him His life. Learning of His faithfulness to them even when they were liars is the only way they'll ever really learn to *love* truth.

Or, consider one more example: generosity. The way you learn to love generosity is by being generous. There have been many times I didn't "feel" like giving away money. I'd get an extra $1,000 and know of some need I should give it to but "felt" like buying a flat screen TV instead. When I gave away the money, however, I experienced the joy of giving. Being generous created in me a desire to be more generous.

Is that compromising gospel-centered change? Am I "adding something to the gospel" by saying you'll become generous both by faith in Jesus and by practicing generosity? Not at all. After all, Jesus Himself said, "Where your treasure is, there your heart will be also" (Matt. 6:21). Do you see what came first in that sequence? You put your treasure somewhere, and *then* your heart follows.

You say, "But isn't gospel-centered generosity being so overwhelmed to the lavish grace of Christ that you delight in being generous?" (see 2 Cor. 8:9). Well, yeah. But actually being generous puts you in touch with the heart of God and as you experience Him, you'll learn to love Him and His ways. Don't try to be more gospel-centered than Jesus. He understood how gospel-centeredness works.

> Our obedience to God when we don't feel like it can even be an act of faith in and of itself.

Our obedience to God when we don't feel like it can even be an act of faith in and of itself, as our act of obedience is a cry to God for Christ's sake to change our hearts so that we desire to obey. That certainly has more faith in it than *not* obeying.

Scripture tells us, in fact, that we are to be actively pursuing the mortification of our flesh (Rom. 6:1–14). *Mortify* implies that we are acting in direct defiance of what our flesh desires. But how exactly do we "mortify the deeds of the flesh?" Paul's answer is by believing we have been made alive in Christ. When our flesh desires that which is contrary to the will of God, we are to believe what God has declared over us in the gospel, and by so doing expunge our hearts from its deadly attraction to sin. Grasping the God revealed in the gospel produces the "new affection" strong enough to snap our addiction to the lesser pleasures. As John Owen said, "Spiritual disciplines can trim the roots of sin, but only the gospel pulls up the roots."

What, Then, Is Legalism?

Isn't legalism any time you teach change through external obedience? Not exactly. Legalism is either when you (a) feel closer to God when you do them, or (b) you put so much emphasis on developing the outward behavior that you neglect the inward change that comes only through faith in the gospel.

Legalism, for example, is thinking that reading the Bible makes God love and accept you more. It does not. Christ kept the law perfectly for me, and reading the Bible for four hours every morning would not make God look any more favorably upon me.

> A gospel-centered approach to reading the Bible means that you discipline yourself to read the Bible even when you don't feel like it.

Legalism is also thinking that forcing myself to read the Bible is sufficient, in and of itself, to generate in my heart a love for God and His Word. Reading the Bible can't do that either; only the Spirit of God does that through the message of the gospel. Reading the Bible does, however, provide an *opportunity* for the Spirit to confront me with the message. As Paul Miller says, "Reading the Bible doesn't create intimacy with God, but it does make room for it."[4]

A gospel-centered approach to reading the Bible means that you discipline yourself to read the Bible even when you don't feel like it, all the while repenting to God that you don't love Him more and saturating your mind with the message that God's acceptance of you is given as a gift in Christ.

Case Study: Fasting

One final example I'll use to really try to drive this home: fasting. Fasting is something I rarely "feel" like doing. In fact, my body never "feels" like doing without food. When you fast, you are actually depriving your body of a legitimate craving so that you can train yourself that satisfying your soul in God is more satisfying than satisfying your body with food.

Fasting, on the surface, looks quite legalistic. How does depriving your body of food produce true spiritual fruit? It doesn't, by itself. Going without food certainly doesn't make you more pleasing to God. But if you use the absence of food to train your soul to feast on the glories of the gospel, fasting becomes a pipe through which the power of the gospel can flow. That's apparently what Jesus did when He fasted. He starved His body from food so He could really understand that "Man shall not live [read: "thrive, come alive"] by bread alone, but by every word that comes from the mouth of God" (Matt. 4:4).[5]

In other words, fasting creates the opportunity to exercise more effective faith in the gospel. The gospel is the only place where the power of new life—the power to develop a love for God and for oth-

> The New Testament does indeed contain imperatives, but they are shrouded in the indicative of the gospel.

ers—resides. The power of the gospel is only released as we believe it. Fasting merely provides us a better opportunity to focus on the gospel and believe it.[6]

So, the New Testament does indeed contain imperatives, but they are shrouded in the indicative of the gospel. The gospel writers do tell us what we are to do for God, but only as they inundate us with the truth about what God has done for us.

Understand the gospel; practice the disciplines

Spiritual disciplines only turn into legalism if you don't really *get* the gospel. If you are thoroughly saturated in the gospel, however, you will practice spiritual disciplines correctly.

Unfortunately, most Christians gravitate toward spiritual disciplines *before* they understand the gospel. The result is a cycle of pride and despair.

A very sincere pastor friend explained to me that he taught the people in his church to conceptualize their Christian growth as the spokes of a wheel. Each spoke represented one of the spiritual disciplines—prayer, faithfulness in Bible reading and church, generosity, witness, community, etc. He then told them, "Rate yourself 1 to 10 on how well you're doing in this area, and draw the length of the spoke to correspond to that number." The resulting picture, he told them, should give them a sense of why their lives were so out of whack spiritually. "So," he told them, "resolve to grow this year in whatever area you are the shortest."

Such a tool can be useful (we even use a version of it at our church!), but only if it is thoroughly saturated in gospel theology. If it's not, then we start to base our spiritual identity on how well we are doing spiritually rather than on what God has declared over us in Christ. Jesus kept all the spiritual disciplines perfectly, in our place, and God judges us now based on His performance, not ours. Spiritual disciplines apart from thorough gospel theology will lead to pride and independence from God *every single time*.

If you understand the gospel, however, then you can practice the spiritual disciplines as God intends: as gateways to the gospel, not as substitutes for the gospel. You can even set goals—for example, to spend at least fifteen minutes in the Word and fifteen minutes in prayer twice every day; to fast once a month; to share Christ weekly, etc. Rather than being sources of pride or despair, those things will simply create

> *If you understand the gospel, you can practice the spiritual disciplines as God intends.*

for you a regular opportunity to interact with the gospel. Even our failures in these areas remind us that God bases His acceptance of us on Christ's keeping of the law, not on ours.

That realization will drive us to stand even more in awe of the grace of God, which will produce even more spiritual fruit.

The more we taste of the gospel, the more we love it. And the more we learn to love the things of God, the more time we'll spend time doing those things, less by discipline and more by desire. We enter into a self-reproducing cycle of life. We are sowing to the Spirit, and from the Spirit reaping life everlasting.

We will be "abiding in Jesus" just as Jesus commanded, and we will bear much fruit, just as He promised.

CHAPTER 13

What Is the Right Way to Work for God?

At the beginning of this book, I told you that I've had a constant struggle figuring out what God wanted from me in light of the needs of the world. The question ringing in my mind, constantly, was: Am I doing enough for God?

The gospel teaches us that our approval by God is not based on doing "enough" for Him. Some might conclude, then, that we have no obligations to the world. The gospel isn't about work, after all; it's about resting in God's work on your behalf.

It's clear though, that Jesus expects His followers to be fervently at work in His kingdom. And if we love people like He's loved us, than we cannot sit idly by while people perish.

But how much is enough? And is it possible to take on too much responsibility? Is enjoying any luxury here on earth a failure to really embrace the sacrificial call of the cross?

In short, I'm asking this: What does a gospel-centered approach to the brokenness of the world look like?

This is an important question to ask, because if we get it wrong, we'll either waste our lives in meaningless pursuits because we don't think we need to do anything for God; or, we'll burn ourselves out carrying a load Jesus never intended us to carry. But if we get it right, we will have the joy of leveraging our lives for Jesus as He leveraged His for us.

A House for God, by God

King David learned the answer to this question when he purposed in his heart to build a temple for God (2 Sam. 7). By this point in David's life God had thoroughly established David as the king of Israel. He had given him a stable kingdom and had defeated all of David's enemies. The land of Israel was prospering and at rest.

As 2 Samuel 7 opens, David is sitting together after dinner with Nathan, the nation's pastor, out on David's back porch. David's eyes fell onto the tabernacle, a ramshackle tent God had His people assemble in which His presence dwelt as they travelled from Egypt.

By this time, the tabernacle was a few hundred years old. It was probably getting pretty threadbare. Plus, it was just a tent, and David's house had just been auditioned for MTV *Cribs.* So David says to Nathan, "You know, this isn't right . . . I live in a nice house that smells like cedar, and God lives in a tent."

Nathan responds like any pastor does when someone wealthy offers to give him money: "Go, my brother, and do all that is in your heart" (2 Sam. 7:3 author paraphrase).

Later that night, however, God appears to Nathan:

> *"Go and tell my servant David, 'Thus says the LORD: Would you build me a house to dwell in? I have not lived in a house since the day I brought up the people of Israel from Egypt to this day, but I have been moving about in a tent for my dwelling. In all places where I have moved with all the people of Israel, did I speak a word . . . saying, "Why have you not built me a house of cedar?"'" (vv. 5–10)*

I think there is a certain playfulness in God's reply. "Ohh . . . so you're going to build ME a house, are you, David? David, you really think I'm worried about My accommodations down there? David, have I ever said, 'I'm tired of this drafty old tent?' You think I want a cedar house? Cedar is for hamsters, David. My streets are made of gold. You have no idea what My real house looks like up here. And if I really needed a nice place to live, David, I wouldn't be coming to you asking you to spot Me some money to build one. After all, remember that . . ."

> "I took YOU *from the pasture, from following the sheep, that you should be prince over my people Israel. And* I have been *with you wherever you went and* have cut off all YOUR enemies *from before you. And* I will make for you a great name. . . . *And* I will appoint a place for my people Israel and will plant them, *so that they may*

dwell in their own place and be disturbed no more. . . . And I will give you rest *from all your enemies. Moreover, the* LORD *declares to you that* the LORD will make you a house." *(vv. 8–11, emphasis mine)*

Who is the featured builder in these verses? Not David— *God.*

God says, "This whole thing is not about you giving to Me, David. This is about Me giving to you. This is not about you building Me a house; I'm building *you* one. I'm the giver; you're the receiver . . . David, I'm not sitting around in heaven going, 'Oh . . . if David would just spare Me a little of his extra money I could get out of these squalid living conditions and build Myself a real kingdom.' *I* created all of this, David, and I don't *need* anything from you in the process. I'm the God who has *everything* and *needs* nothing. I will build this house, and I don't *need* one ounce of your help in the process."

God then goes on to tell David about the Messiah He will send who would build His house on earth. That Messiah, of course, would be God Himself in the flesh. God would build the house of salvation on earth, and David was not *needed*, in the sense that David was supplying something to God that He didn't already have.

God then says,

"And your house and your kingdom shall be made sure forever before me. Your throne shall be established forever."
. . . Then King David went in and sat before the LORD *and said, "Who am I, O Lord* GOD, *and what is my house, that you have brought me thus far? And yet this was a*

small thing in your eyes, O Lord GOD. . . . And what more can David say to you? . . . Because of your promise, and according to your own heart, you have brought about all this greatness, to make your servant know it." (2 Sam. 7:16, 18–21)

Consider this: David started this discussion wanting to build something for God. He ends it sitting in awe of what God is doing for Him.

Isn't this the recurring theme of the gospel? Salvation is not primarily about us doing something for God. Salvation is about *knowing* what God has done for us—and sitting in stunned awe of it. This is pivotal for us to remember as we consider the right way to work for God.

> In Christianity we will do things for God. But what we do will be a grateful response to what He's done for us, not because He needs our help.

Yes, in Christianity we will do things for God. But what we do will be a grateful response to what He's done for us, not because He *needs* our help.

Slow down and read that statement again.

So David says: "Therefore you are great, O LORD God" (2 Sam. 7:22, emphasis mine).

Again, who is great? David, because he built for God a magnificent house? No. God is great, because He did for

David what David could never do for himself. God built
David a house from nothing.

> *"For there is none like you, and there is no God besides you.*
> *. . . And who is like* your people Israel, *the one nation*
> *on earth whom God went to redeem to be his people,*
> *making himself a name and doing for them great and*
> *awesome things by driving out before your people, whom*
> *you redeemed for yourself from Egypt, a nation and its*
> *gods?. . . And your name will be magnified forever."*
> *(vv. 22–23, 26, emphasis mine)*

God's name will be magnified forever because of what
God did on earth. The world is not supposed to look at
Christians and primarily say, *"Wow, what great and impressive*
things they have done for God," but *"Wow, what great things God*
has done for them."

What should stand out about us as people look at us is
the grace and power of *Christ* that exudes from our lives.
Christian witness is primarily a testimony about God's work
on our behalf, not about our work on His.

As David acknowledged in his prayer, God set the pattern for how His work was to be done in the first great act
of salvation, the Exodus.
The Exodus did not put
on display all the great
and impressive things that
Israel had done for God.
The Exodus makes you

> *Christian witness is*
> *primarily a testimony*
> *about God's work on our*
> *behalf, not about our*
> *work on His.*

stand in awe of the amazing things that God had done for Israel.

Moses, if you recall, was a most unlikely leader. He was basically a shepherd with a lisp, charged with pioneering the greatest political movement of all time. Most people have totally the wrong idea about Moses. We think of a 6'4" basketball team captain with a deep, baritone, Charlton Heston-esque voice who booms out to Pharoah, "God says, '*Let My people go!*'" and everyone cowers beneath the power of Moses' persona. One of the few personal things we *know* about Moses was that he was "weak in speech," which means that his oral presentation left much to be desired. Maybe he had a little mousy voice, or maybe he stuttered. Whatever it was, when he showed up in Pharoah's court to demand Israel's release, no one took him seriously.

> God hangs a sign outside of the construction zone of His kingdom that says "No help needed."

But then the plagues started. One by one all of Egypt's strongholds were shattered. The mighty Nile was turned to blood. The sun was darkened. Flies overtook the land. The firstborn son of every unprotected household died.

As Israel walked out of Egypt that day to freedom, no one said, "Wow, Moses is quite the leader." Nor did they marvel at what an incredible people this group of slaves were. Rather, they stood in awe at what God had done for them.

That's how Christians in every generation are to be. The house of salvation is not built by us, for God; but by God, for us. God hangs a sign outside of the construction zone of His kingdom that says "*No* help needed."

The Work Principle

What does this teach us about our responsibility in working for God to complete His mission on earth?

God doesn't need us.

God builds a house for us; He is not looking to us to build one for him. Salvation, start to finish, is from God, and He doesn't need anything from us in the process.

Jesus went to the cross *alone*. The cross was not a team effort. Everyone abandoned Jesus at the cross. Like David had done, Jesus ran out onto that field alone to face the giant of our sin while we all stood in unfaithfulness on the sidelines.

When Jesus was raised from the dead, it was by God's power alone, with no help from any of us. The disciples weren't beside Him with their crash carts going, "Come on, Jesus . . . More mouth to mouth, Peter. John, give him another electric shock." The Father brought Jesus back from the dead *all by Himself.*

When Jesus establishes His eternal kingdom on earth in the future, it is something the Bible says He will do by Himself. The book of Revelation says that the New Jerusalem comes down to earth from heaven, prepared by God for us. We don't build it up to heaven from the earth for Him.

In the same way, it is God alone who can build His church on the earth today. When Jesus sent His disciples out to complete the Great Commission (Matt. 16:18), He said to them,

"*I* will build my church, and the gates of hell shall not prevail against it," not "You will build My church, and I'll be around to assist you when you need help."

Imagine how overwhelming it was when Jesus lays the Great Commission on the disciples. "Basically, you must take the gospel to every person in every country in the world because I am the only way they can be saved and you are the only way they can hear about Me" (Acts 1:6–8).

Big mission. Lots of work involved. Better get started working right away. Surprisingly, however, the first thing Jesus told them to do is go and wait. Do nothing. Nothing, that is, but wait for the coming of the Holy Spirit. I am sure the more type A of the disciples were like, "*Wait*? We need to get organized! We need to raise money. We need to train up preachers. Time is wasting! People are dying! We must go *now*!" Jesus understood their feeling, no doubt, but He still told them to wait. Why did He tell them that? *If nothing else, Jesus was drilling into them that He alone can build His church and complete the Great Commission.* They were powerless to bring about world salvation. "Apart from Me," He had told them, "you can do *nothing*."

The point screamed from cover to cover in the Bible is "God doesn't *need* you for anything." You and I are utterly powerless to bring about salvation and healing. This message is at the core of the gospel. The gospel aims to shatter pride and independence from every angle. The gospel's first work is to make us to sit in stunned awe at what God has done for us.

Now . . . you say, "Wait a minute. God doesn't *need* me? Then does that mean I should go about my merry way spending all my money on myself, sitting back waiting on *God* to feed the poor and win the lost?"

Not at all. Because here is the second part of the giving principle:

As recipients of grace, we will want to give back to God.

When we grasp how much God has given to us in grace, and we see how great the needs of the world are, we will *want* to work for God.

God told David he had the right attitude—just the wrong plan. David saw how much God had done for Him, and he wanted to do something in return. David wanted all the people in Israel to know that God was the hero behind his success. The temple he wanted to build should direct people's attention to the greatness of God. God commended David:

> *When we think about how many people in the world are dying, both body and soul, without God, we want to see the grace that has been given to us come to them also.*

"Because it was in your heart to build a house for My name, you did well that it was in your heart" (2 Chron. 6:8 NASB).

So after being told "no" to building, David set about to collecting all the materials and plans for the temple so Solomon would have what he needed to build it (1 Chron. 22:1–6). After what God had done for David, he wanted to do *something*! Even though God didn't technically need him to help build the temple, David wanted to do something for the God who had done so much for him.

In response to the gospel, we should want to give back to God. Think about it: where would you be without Jesus?

And when we think about how many people in the world are dying, both body and soul, without God, we want to see the grace that has been given to us come to them also. What else would a gospel-centered person *want* to do with their resources?

We must offer ourselves to God and do what He leads us to do.

When we put those first two principles together, we arrive at the third: gospel-centered people offer themselves to God, joyfully, and then do whatever He directs them to do, knowing that only what He empowers them to do will do any real good. *That's* what we are responsible for—offering *all* we have to God and asking for His direction. That's exactly what David did.

You see a clear picture of what this looks like in Acts. After the Holy Spirit came, the disciples didn't sit back on the couch and say, "Wow . . . Glad You're here, Holy Spirit. Let us know when world evangelization is done. We're going fishing." Instead, they said, "Here am I, send me!" They prayed for God to empower them and send them. They asked God to use them. They knew that if God didn't send them, they were powerless to do any good. In response to the gospel, however, they begged to be sent. They wanted to be poured out for others as Jesus had been poured out for them, but not from some idolatrous, man-glorifying notion that they could build the kingdom of God on their own.

The weight of saving the world is not on our shoulders. We couldn't handle if it was. And we really couldn't do anything about it anyway. God alone saves. God provides. In response to the gospel, however, we offer ourselves fully to God, longing for world salvation. Then we do whatever He directs us to do. Those who place *all* of their resources at the disposal of Jesus in grateful response to His grace and with great confidence in

> *Those who place* all *of their resources at the disposal of Jesus will find nearly unlimited power at their disposal.*

His ability will find nearly unlimited power at their disposal. Just think of the story of the boy with five loaves and two fish (John 6:1–15) or the woman who gave the two coins (Luke 21:1–4). God didn't need what they provided. In fact, the little boy went home with more than he gave. But 5,000 plus people were fed in the process.

Hearing from Nathan

You say, "Well, that's great . . . But I've never had a Nathan who had a dream where God told him what I was supposed to do. How am I supposed to know how God wants me to work for Him?"[1]

Technically, God never told David to collect the stuff for the temple. David just started doing it, and God didn't stop him.

So here are a few thoughts to help you get started in what you should be doing for God:

1. *Start with the needs right in front of you.* The book of
   James says that if someone is standing at your door
   with a need, then it is God's intention for you to fill
   it. The idea that "God doesn't need us" should never
   be used as an excuse to not meet the needs that are
   right in front of us. Jesus praised the Good Samaritan
   in the parable because he met the need when he saw
   it, and criticized the priest and the Levite who passed
   the man by, feeling "called" to higher things. So, start
   by helping those in need "right outside of your gates."
   If there is a need that you see you can fulfill, do it.²

2. *Carefully evaluate how your vocational talents can be
   leveraged for God's kingdom.* How can your job be
   leveraged to bless others?³ One of the most underuti-
   lized tools in discerning what God wants you to do is
   the local church. Just as God used Nathan, who was
   part of David's spiritual community, to direct David,
   so God will use His local church to help direct you.

3. *Ask what your local church is doing that you can be
   involved in.* God has given us our local churches to
   help direct us in effectively meeting the spiritual and
   physical needs of our city. If your church doesn't have
   a ministry to its city, go to a new one.

4. *Consider whether there is some area of passion or interest growing in you.* What stirs your heart? Is there
   a people group, or a country, you think about all
   the time? Do you have a dream of doing something
   particularly great for God? Commit that to God,
   and ask Him to send you. Wait on Him to open the
   door (Ps. 37:4–5). Don't be afraid to (in the words of

William Carey), "Expect great things of God, and
then attempt great things for God." God can tell you
"no" if He needs to, but often the dream itself is from
Him. A lot of times the way we discover our spiritual
gifts is by sensing a deep desire in our hearts to do
something for others for Christ's sake.

5. *Listen to what other believers say about your gifted-
    ness.* Often, God reveals areas of spiritual-giftedness
    in us by having someone from the church point it out
    to us. Other people see an area where we are particu-
    larly strong, or where God has used us in their lives.
    That's how I discovered my gift of preaching. Other
    people told me how much God used me in their lives
    when I'd teach God's word.

6. *Be open to the guidance of the Holy Spirit.* Just as God
    got a message to Nathan, He can get one to you.
    It might come in the form of a word of prophecy
    someone speaks to you, the counsel of a wise friend,
    a closed door, or anything else God chooses to use.
    God's not new at this communication thing. He can
    get His message to you. You can trust Him.

God is the master builder of His house, and you and
I only lowly footsoldiers. We simply carry out orders; He pro-
vides the resources. He will tell us what He wants us to do.
Then we do it with what He's provided.

David's son Solomon, whom God used to build the
earthly version of the temple David had himself wanted to
build, probably said it best: "Unless the Lord builds the house,
those who build it labor in vain" (Ps. 127:1).

We should eagerly yearn for God to build His house through us and wait expectantly on Him to use us in the process. But eagerly offering ourselves to God is not the same as rushing out to it for Him. Contrary to popular opinion, the Great Commission does not begin with "Go into all the world and preach the gospel." The Great Commission begins with "All authority has been given to Me in heaven and on earth" (Matt. 28:18 NKJV). Before Jesus gives the Great Commission, He reminds the apostles that ultimately the Great Commission is His. He is the One with the ability to build the church, and He is the One who must do it through us. As Michael Horton says: "The Great Commission begins with the Great Announcement."[4]

Only by believing in the sufficiency of the God of the Great Announcement will we ever have the confidence to attempt bold things for the Great Commission.

So, ask God earnestly to be used by Him, and then do whatever He puts in front of you with the confidence that He is doing it through you. That is the only right way to work for God.

CHAPTER 14

What Does a Gospel-Centered Church Look Like?

Here's where it gets really exciting. It's one thing for an individual to have a reawakening to the greatness of the gospel. It takes it to another level for an entire church to experience something like this. Can you imagine the kind of witness hundreds of people living gospel-centered lives together in a local church might have in a community? Can you fathom the kind of mercy and grace that would exude from their fellowship, and the kind of impact they would have when they began to be to their community as Jesus was to them? And what it looks like when an entire church of people begins to sense God's willingness and ability to save their community, and ask accordingly? I get excited just writing that.

So let's get right to the heart of the issue: What does a gospel-centered church look like?

I'm going to give you three qualities of a "gospel-centered" church. Unfortunately, I think the examples of churches who model all three are very few.

1. *In a gospel-centered church, preaching the message of the gospel is the priority.* The gospel is an announcement, not about what we are to do for God, but about what He has done for us.

Gospel, in Greek, was not an exclusively religious word. It simply meant "good news." When a Greek king would win a battle, he would send a "gospel carrier" around Greece to announce that he had won the battle, was in control again, and that the people were free. When that announcement was made, the people were expected to believe it and live accordingly.

The gospel is an announcement that Jesus is Lord and that He has won the battle for your salvation. We are to respond in repentance and faith (Mark 1:15). The gospel is not *good advice* about how to live; it is *good news* about what God has done.

Jesus told His disciples to "be His witnesses," which meant they were to tell everyone, faithfully, the story of what *He had done* for the world. Their lives would certainly demonstrate the changes His power brought in their lives, but they were to constantly point to what He had done that made those changes possible.

> *The gospel is not* good advice *about how to live; it is* good news *about what God has done.*

Where there is no proclamation of the story of Jesus Christ, there is no gospel ministry.

Have you ever heard that statement (attributed to Francis of Assisi), "Preach the gospel. If necessary, use words"? How do you explain the gospel without using *words*? That's like saying, "Tell me your phone number. If necessary, use digits." Your phone number *is* digits. The gospel *is* the words announcing what Christ has done. People can't look at our lives and know the story of Christ. They may see glimpses of the kindness of Christ, but expecting them to get the gospel just by watching us would be like trying to gather information from a newscast with the sound turned off.

We are to be always, everywhere, preaching the word. That's what the early church did. Everywhere, from house to house, they were always telling the story of Jesus.

2. *In a gospel-centered church, the emphasis of the message is more on what Christ has done than what we are to do.* As I'm sure you've seen by now, the only thing that brings true spiritual growth is abiding in—dwelling in, thinking about, standing in awe of—what Christ has done for us.

When our message and ministry highlight something besides that, we sever the lifeline between people and the power of God, no matter how "good" and useful the thing we are preaching about is. *Nothing* we are to do for God is as important as what He has done for us.

As I look across the Christian landscape, I see churches emphasizing all kinds of *good* things that unfortunately keep people from focusing on the *essential* thing, the glory and free grace of God revealed in the gospel.

Few of these things they emphasize are bad in and of themselves, they just become bad because they tend to eclipse the one thing that *is itself* the power of God for us—the gospel.

My description below is not meant to caricature various traditions, but it might help you see where various traditions tend to substitute something for the gospel as the primary means of spiritual growth.

At many "charismatic" churches, the emphasis is placed on having an experience with the Spirit. We certainly need to be intimately acquainted with the Spirit. But an experience with the Spirit cannot replace the centrality of the gospel message. In fact, what the Spirit most longs to do is to make the gospel real to our hearts (2 Cor. 3:18–4:4), and the way we are filled by the Spirit is by grasping and believing more of the gospel. In other words, *being filled by the Spirit happens when we renew our minds in the awareness of the gospel, not through a special ceremony*. You want to be filled with the Spirit? Believe the gospel again (Gal. 3:1–3; Acts 10:43–45). When we teach people to seek closeness to God through an ecstatic experience rather than pointing them back to renewed faith in the gospel, we are eclipsing the gospel with a secondary experience. The Spirit Himself would *never* do this. His role is to point us to the glories of the gospel (John 15:26).

At many "seeker-sensitive" churches, the emphasis is on clear, practical action steps for Christian living. "Show them," this idea goes, "how to live this out. Show them how God can fix their marriage. Show them how much better life would be if they would do it God's way." Now, being a type A, task-oriented person, *I love action steps*. Clear action steps cannot change the heart, however. Being told what to do cannot change me; only standing in awe of what God has done can. Learning "five steps toward good communication" will not do nearly as much for my marriage as embracing the billion steps God has taken toward me in Jesus Christ.

Tim Keller has said, "Religion tells you to go and change; the gospel changes you on the spot." Action steps that do not flow out of adoration of Jesus and gratefulness for what He's done will ultimately produce only frustrated, prideful Pharisees, no matter how winsomely those action steps are presented.

At many "fundamentalist" churches, the emphasis is on proper behavior. You always leave knowing how Christians should behave, talk, or dress. To be honest, I don't really have a problem with "guidelines," because—face it—we all have a certain amount of guidelines we expect others to honor. At even the most relaxed churches it is generally understood that girls shouldn't walk around topless, guys shouldn't wear thongs, and deacons shouldn't drop the "f-bomb." The problem is not with guidelines, *per se*; the problem is when the emphasis on those guidelines eclipses the gospel itself. Cleaning up my language cannot change me. *Acting* like a Christian cannot change me. Only being overwhelmed at the God of the gospel can change me. The main problem is not the guidelines themselves (though some of them can be, at times, ridiculous); the problem is in the *emphasis* given to them.

At many "younger" churches, the emphasis is on relaxing the standards of fundamentalism. In our grandparents' churches our spirituality was measured by church attendance; Sunday school; Sunday and Wednesday night services; being at revival; going on weekly visitation; and knowing all forty-seven verses of "Just As I Am." Contemporary churches often just change the list and take off the tie. The new list includes volunteering at one of the weekend services, going to small group, and, above all, tithing. The elements on the list might have changed, but it is still a list of to-do's, and the expectation is still that outward behavior modifications are God's primary way of changing our hearts. A lot of the new, cool, emerging Christianity has turned out simply to be "old legalism" in grunge clothing. Michael Horton says: "For all of the (younger) movement's incisive critiques of the megachurch model, the emphasis still falls on measuring the level of our zeal and activity rather than on immersing people in the greatest story ever told."[1]

At many "Reformed" churches, the particulars of Reformed theology overshadow the cross. The assumption seems to be that if you can master the particulars of the TULIP,[2] and are devoted to 1, 2, and 3 John (John Calvin, John Piper, and John MacArthur), then you are spiritually acceptable and everything will be right in your life. Right doctrine is, of course, essential, but no "doctrinal flower" can transform your heart. Only the beauty of Jesus transforms the heart. I know some will say, "But the five points of Calvinism *are* the essence of the gospel!" Perhaps. But if you emphasize conformity to your version of the five points more than you do a simple worship of the Christ of the cross, you have replaced adoration with information. Right information is essential, but I have seen far too many people who are more excited about the TULIP than they were in awe of the cross. I have also seen many people who don't take my exact stance on the five points who are passionately in love with Jesus and positively overwhelmed at His grace.

At many "prosperity gospel" churches, the emphasis is placed on the victorious, blessed life God wants you to have. I don't have a problem teaching that God loves to bless His children. He does. But what really changes you is not the hope that God can give you more material stuff in the future; what changes you is when you see God Himself is better than any blessing He could give you, and that even if you lose everything and have Him, it is enough. And sometimes God teaches you that by pain and deprivation. The *real* damage of prosperity teaching is that it redirects our eyes away from God to His gifts. When "how God will bless us if we obey" overshadows "the value of the God given to us in the cross," we encourage idolatry and retard true spiritual growth.

At many "discipleship-focused" churches, the emphasis is on a radical, sacrificial commitment to discipleship and generosity. Again, amen. It's true that following Jesus means renouncing all we have, taking up our cross to follow Him, and pouring out our resources for His kingdom. *How though, can we produce a heart of generosity in people, a heart that pours itself for the world because it loves it like God does?* The apostle John said that our radical giving should prove the presence of our love.[3] Love without radical giving is worthless (1 John 3:16–18), he says, but so is radical giving without love (1 Cor. 13:1–3). So our commands to radical living should be shrouded in the announcement of God's love given to us in Christ, because only in that message will we learn to love God (1 John 4:19).

If we only command people to be generous, we will produce merely desperate people who run out to do something extravagantly generous to prove they are saved. That is a type of works-righteousness, in which we try to add a work to our lives to prove we are children of God.

A heart of generosity will only be produced in us as we embrace and believe the gospel. Those people who have tasted the gospel will respond with extravagant generosity. Don't confuse diagnosis with prognosis. Diagnosis is what is wrong; prognosis is how to fix it. If our hearts are calloused and selfish, we can't fix that just by giving money away. We have to become more aware of the extravagant kindness of God toward us in Christ. Selfishness is the diagnosis; the gospel is the primary prognosis.

At many "emergent" churches, the emphasis is on the wholistic nature of salvation, particularly social justice and racial reconciliation issues. Amen. We need to be paying attention to those issues, and gospel-centered Christians will care about them. But you cannot confuse the *effects of* the gospel with the gospel itself. In Galatians 3, Paul said that Jew and Gentile would be brought together as they understood what God had to do to save all of us. When we've been changed by the gospel, we care about the victims of injustice and get involved. These are the effects of the gospel; they are not the gospel itself. Mimicking revolutionary Christians in the first century will not change our hearts; embracing what Jesus did for us in the first century will.

> You cannot confuse the effects of *the gospel* with the gospel itself.

In almost all of the instances above, the problem is not with what's being taught, but with the *emphasis* being given to what is taught. Error, it has been said, is often simply "truth out of proportion."[4] In other words, "heresy" is not just wrong teaching; it is also putting undue emphasis on certain aspects of good teaching. I love how Michael Horton says it: "We can lose Christ by *distraction* as easily as by denial . . . 'Christless Christianity' can happen through addition as well as subtraction."[5]

Gospel-centered churches, then, emphasize most of all the news about what Christ has done for us. The secondary matters *flow out from* that; they don't eclipse it.

3. *In a gospel-centered church, the members demonstrate the beauty of the gospel in the community.* While the gospel is, first and foremost, a message, it is always accompanied by demonstrations of that message. Every time the gospel was preached by Jesus and the earliest apostles, it was followed by "signs." These were more than awe-inspiring magic tricks; signs were miracles with a message. They put the message of God's kingdom on tangible display.

A sign doesn't always have to be miraculous. A sign simply demonstrates the love and beauty of God's kingdom. The church, Paul said, was to be God's "demonstration" community, where He puts on display for a watching world His "manifold wisdom" and incredible power (Eph. 3:10–11, 21).

In Acts, when the early church was simply being "the church," Luke tells us a great sense of fear and "awe came upon every soul," they had "favor with all the people," and "the Lord added to their number day by day those who were being saved" (Acts 2:42–47). In other words, just by doing what healthy local churches do (praying, sharing, constantly preaching the word, etc.), they were evangelizing the community. The presence of a healthy local church in a community

> *The presence of a healthy local church in a community is the greatest catalyst for the evangelization of that community.*

is the greatest catalyst for the evangelization of that community. In a healthy church the local community should see the glory of the gospel on display. As they do, many in the community will be overcome with a sense of fear and awe and many will be moved to believe—just as they were in Acts 2:42–47.

There are at least four things we find in the book of Acts about the church that "amazed" the community. Each of these put the gospel on display. Each of these will be present in a gospel-centered congregation.

The Church and the Book of Acts

Love and unity in the church

The love and unity in the local church amazed the community. It was more than a fraternity of friends; it was an eclectic family with unexpected unity. In an age of dramatic social, class, and racial differences, the local church was the only institution in the Roman world that brought unity between classes and races. The churches Paul planted were diverse fellowships of Jew and Gentile, young and old, poor and rich. Rodney Stark says that this is one of the most significant factors contributing to the early church's explosive growth in the first 400 years following Christ.[6]

Francis Schaeffer famously called the church God's "final apologetic" to a skeptical world. That's because in the church the world sees a unity that staggers the mind; that shows that all people have a common ancestry (God); a common problem (sin); and a common Savior (Jesus).

> The church is God's "final apologetic" to a skeptical world.

Generosity

The radical generosity of the church amazed the community, and it drew attention to the radical generosity of Christ. Emperor Julian, one of Christianity's fiercest persecutors, complained in a letter to a friend that he just could not keep the church from growing, no matter what he did. In disgust, he said, *"The godless Galileans! They take care not only of their own poor, but ours as well."* It was Christians giving themselves away to those unable to pay them back that convinced a skeptical Roman world the truth of Jesus' claims. I've come to see that in my own community too. I live in what *Forbes* magazine calls "the educational hub of America." Skepticism often accompanies education. In our community, extravagant generosity has often been more convincing than our philosophical reasoning (which is not to say we don't also often present ready, reasonable answers to the Christian faith!).

> In a post-Christian, skeptical age, love on display is sometimes the most convincing apologetic.

In a post-Christian, skeptical age, love on display is the most convincing apologetic.

In the early church, no one went hungry. No one went without shelter. Everyone was provided for. People sold fields, provided food, and went broke for the sake of others. The surrounding community was amazed. And they believed.

Joy in the midst of persecution

The joy with which the early church suffered also amazed people. Their willingness to speak about Jesus when it cost them everything was confounding to the casual observer (Acts 4:13). Their ability to have joy in the midst of great pain drew people's attention to the value they placed on God. Anybody can be happy when things are going well. When Paul was held captive unjustly in a Philippian prison, however, his back still raw from the beating the night before, and praising God rather than cursing God or vowing vengeance, the skeptical Philippian jailor took notice (Acts 16:25–31).

I was watching TV one morning with my five-year-old when a preacher with a smile the size of Texas came on and explained to his viewers that if they would give him a "seed gift" of $1,500, God would for certain multiply His blessings back on them. He urged viewers who were in credit card debt to fill up the last bit of space on their credit cards making a donation to him. "God might reward you with a BMW," he said, "and your neighbors will be amazed at the smile you have on your face as you pull in and out of your garage in your new car, and you can tell them the great news about what Jesus has done for you."

Really? Your neighbors will be *amazed* at the smile on your face when you are driving your new BMW? I suspect anyone would smile in that circumstance. What will amaze your friends is when your body is racked with cancer and your 401K investments have tanked and you are still able to say, "I have a hope and joy in God beyond the reach of all these things." When our circumstances are the darkest, the light of our hope in God shines the brightest.

Miraculous answer to prayer

Last but not least, the miraculous answers God gave to the prayers of the early church amazed the community. Miraculous answers to prayer are not just something God did in Apostalic times. Don't write those off as a relic of the past. God said repeatedly throughout the Bible that what would distinguish His people was the way He answered their prayers (Deut. 4:7). Perhaps the only reason we don't see God move in our midst like they did was we don't ask Him like they did.[7]

Thirty-nine out of forty miracles in the book of Acts happen *outside* the church, in the community. I often tell our church that means I, as a pastor, have access to only 1/40 of the power of God, since I spend most of my time in the church! Most of it waits for them. God's power is ready to be manifested in the community. He wants to demonstrate in our city that He is willing and able to save.

When I lived among Muslims in Southeast Asia, there were times I just didn't know what to do or say to make Jesus known to them. So I'd offered to pray for sick people. I laid my hands on dozens of people and prayed for them in Jesus' name. Some of them got better. I'll never forget the day a group of 12-year-old boys rang my doorbell so one could ask me to pray for his mother. I heard a kid in the back of the group say, "Why are you asking him to come? He's not a Muslim." The other boy said, "Yes, but this is a man God listens to."

God often authenticates His message in a community through miraculous answers to the prayers of the church in that community.

The Signs Accentuate the Message, Not Replace It

Love and unity. Generosity. Joy in persecution. Miraculous answers to prayer. These are amazing things. But we must again remember: these amazing works accentuate, but can never replace, the verbal explanation of the gospel. Our generosity, joy, love, and miraculous power only put on display the glorious gospel we proclaim with our words. They cannot replace preaching. Signs are only good if it is clear what they are signifying.

Whenever any good work, no matter how worthy it was in itself, got in the way of the preaching of the message, Jesus and the apostles ceased it immediately. That is because the signs were to point to the message. If they were distracting from the message, they were no longer serving their purpose.

> *Whenever any good work got in the way of the preaching of the message, Jesus and the apostles ceased it immediately.*

For example, after Jesus miraculously fed the 5,000 with the five loaves and two fishes, the people became fixated on Jesus' ability to immediately end world hunger. They wanted to make Him king right then and there. What was Jesus' response? Start a worldwide "end hunger" crusade? No, He refused to repeat the miracle and preached instead to the people about the need to see Him as the Bread of Life (John 6:26–27).

Jesus was once asked by a man to help him resolve a property dispute with his other brother. The guy had a legitimate justice complaint. As we know, God is concerned about justice (Isa. 58; Amos 4:6–8). Yet, in that situation, Jesus refused to intervene, saying that this was not really "His business." Instead, He preached a sermon to both of them about the sin of greed. Jesus' "business," first and foremost, was to confront hearts with their need for the gospel (Luke 12:13–14).

In Acts 6, the apostles were presented with a legitimate social need in their community—the widows needed someone to help put food on their tables. The apostles responded that others would have to see to this concern because they could not be distracted from preaching, their most important task (Acts 6:1–5).

D. Martyn Lloyd-Jones said this about that story:

> Can't you hear people during that time say, "What good is preaching if people among us are starving and suffering? The time for preaching is over and the time for action is here." However, the Apostles, under the influence of the Holy Spirit, saw the dangerous temptation put in front of them and said, "Nothing can

eclipse the importance of preaching the Word. We'll ask God to help us raise up others who can meet those needs. We cannot, by any means, quit preaching."[8]

Nothing, no matter how good or urgent, can keep us from pursuing our primary objective: *preaching the gospel.* But as we are preaching it, our lives should be putting the love, peace, and joy of the gospel on graphic display. Our community should taste in us the love of Christ in a way that leaves them amazed, and hungry for more.

> *Nothing, no matter how good or urgent, can keep us from pursuing our primary objective:* preaching the gospel.

Does your life do that? When is the last time someone was amazed by your generosity? When is the last time they asked you where the joy you possess in suffering could possibly come from?

Is your church doing that in your community?

How one middle-class church has learned to put the gospel on display

In 2004, God convicted our church that we were not putting on display the generosity of the gospel in our community. I was teaching through the first half of the book of Acts, and we came to Acts 8:6–8 where it says, "The crowds with one accord paid attention to what was being said by Philip when they heard him and saw the signs that he did. . . . So there was much joy in that city."

I asked our church if they thought there was "much joy" in the city as a result of our presence there. Then I read the story in Acts 9 about Tabitha (who had the toughest nickname of the New Testament: "Dorcas") who had done so many good works and acts of charity that when she died the community gathered at her bedside and wept. I asked our church, "Do you think if the Summit Church 'died' that our community would weep that we were gone?"

We believed the answer to both those questions was "no." If anything, the community may have been excited that we were gone because they would regain access to our tax-exempt piece of property and get less "junk" mail cluttering their mailbox (though I certainly don't want to underestimate the significance of the people who trusted Christ at our church and the joy present in their lives during that time).

To make a long story short, we resolved that with God's help we would become a blessing to our city—to incarnate Christ's love to them. To bring His love and His healing to the places in our city that needed Him most. So we asked God to show us ways we could demonstrate the peace and love of the kingdom to them.

Shortly thereafter, God brought to our attention a very underperforming public elementary school in the inner city. The school was the worst ranked school in our county and was on track to be shut down within two years.

Over the next several years we became very involved with that school. We led in several renovation projects. Many of our people got involved tutoring children. Small groups adopted classrooms and teachers, housed refugees, and met physical needs of families in the school. One soon-to-be-married couple in our church asked that any gifts for them be redirected to a family in the school whose house had been destroyed in a fire.

At the end of that first year, the principal asked us if we would pray for her students during end-of-the-year exams because their scores would be the primary criteria by which the school would be evaluated.

In the fourth year of our involvement, the school (which previously had the lowest scores of any school in the county) had the highest percentage of kids to pass their end-of-year exams. In a report chronicling our involvement with the school, the principal credited the church's efforts with helping to improve the school's academic performance.[9] At a teacher's banquet shortly thereafter, one of the teachers said, "I have always known you Christians believed you should love your neighbor. . . . I've never known what it looked like until now."

This past January I was invited to speak at our city's annual Martin Luther King, Jr. rally. It is a very significant event in our city—televised, with all city and county government officials present. They asked me simply to explain why we thought it was important to love the community.

Just a few minutes before the program started, I was standing backstage as nervous as Joel Osteen at an Acts 29 event. The county manager, sensing my anxiety, put his hand on my shoulder and said, "J.D., do you know why you've been asked to speak at this event?"

I said, "No, and if you could tell me I'd really appreciate it, because I'm super nervous."

He said, "Because of all your church has done for our city."

Later I was told, "Everywhere in our city we find a need, we also find people from the Summit Church meeting that need. We couldn't think of anyone to better embody the spirit of brotherly love in our city than you, on behalf of your church." I went out that day and for twenty minutes explained that our church's generosity was a response to the radical generosity of Christ toward us. Christ had done for us what we could not do for ourselves; how could we not extend that to those who are in need? At the end of my time the school board, mayor, and city council gave a standing ovation.

The works substantiate the message. They make it visible and understandable.

Over the last few years, I've heard so many stories in our church of small groups taking up money to pay for people's surgeries; housing refugees; even downsizing houses in order to give more away. We've had guests remark how generously and respectfully they were treated when they came onto our church campus.

It is our joy to say to people when they ask the reason behind our generosity: "We love to be generous to others because Christ has been so generous to us." Our generosity provides us the opportunity to proclaim the gospel. Our kindness to the people of our city is only a dim shadow of Jesus' great kindness of us, but I believe it has helped people in our city to understand more of what Jesus is like. It has helped create in our community a hunger for the gospel.

Preach the gospel, to all people in all times at all places!

A gospel-centered church prioritizes the message of the gospel in its ministries; focuses that message on what Christ has done rather than anything we are to be doing, and then demonstrates the gospel in the community around them.

A gospel-centered church is always about the gospel. It preaches the gospel in all places, at all times, to all people. The gospel is the defining element in every part of their ministry.

Nonbelievers need to hear the gospel to believe it and be saved. Believers need to be reminded of the gospel so they can grow deeper in Christ. There is really no distinction, you see, between what believers need to hear and what unbelievers need to hear. Both believers and unbelievers need to get a glimpse of God's majestic glory, a taste of His surpassing beauty, and a sense of how much grace God has shown toward them in Christ. Both believers and unbelievers need to be rebuked for their pride and self-sufficiency, to be reminded of the all-surpassing beauty of God. They both need to be stirred up to faith. The gospel is the center of the message no matter who you are talking to. It is everything. Christ is all.

So make the gospel central in everything you do. Preach it everywhere. Always. To everyone.

You'll Never Find the Bottom

One of the things I love about Jesus' stories is that He often uses rather shady characters to make His point. Such is the case in the parable of the treasure hidden in a field, recorded in Matthew 13:44.

In it, a man is ambling along through a buddy's field when he stubs his toe on what he assumes to be a rock protruding from the dirt. He digs a little with his hands, and discovers that this is no rock; this is the corner of a great treasure chest filled with vintage Elvis memorabilia of tremendous value. Rather than telling his buddy about what he's found, however, he re-hides the treasure and makes an offer on the field. His buddy (who is completely ignorant about the treasure) asks why he wants to buy it, and the man says, "Oh, I don't know . . . the grass and the dirt and the trees are so . . . pretty . . . I don't know . . . I just want it." Because his friend has no reason to sell the field, he quotes him an astronomical price.

Before he can even get the figure out of his mouth, however, the man screams "SOLD!" and rushes home to pull together his money. The problem is that he doesn't have that kind of money on hand, so he has to liquidate everything. He does a massive yard sale and borrows money from whoever will lend it. He gives up literally everything. But Jesus describes the man's attitude toward this whole affair with one word: "joy."

> In his joy he goes and sells all that he has and buys that field. (13:44)

What fills his heart is not sorrow for what he's losing, but joy for what he's gaining. The man skips all the way to the bank to divest himself of all his assets because he knows that what he is gaining is infinitely more valuable than anything he is giving up.

Jesus said that finding God is like that. Make no mistake—to follow Jesus means that you relinquish your right to everything else in the world. You literally must renounce it all (Luke 14:33). That means nothing can be off-limits to Jesus. You cannot put limits on where you will live or what you will do. Your "contract" with Him can have no stipulations; it is absolute, unconditional surrender. You must be willing to depart from family, friends, comforts, riches, and even your own life. You must be willing to then pick up His rough, painful, wooden cross and follow Him. You must live for others as He has lived for you.

But if you perceive the value of Jesus, none of this will seem like sacrifice. The cross is painful and the costs of discipleship are severe, but the joy of what you have obtained in Him so far outweighs any sorrow for what you have abandoned.

Hebrews 12:2 says that Jesus went to the cross with joy.

"Who for the joy that was set before him endured the cross, despising the shame, and is seated at the right hand of the throne of God."

He certainly didn't love the cross, the author of Hebrews said. He had to endure it. Its pain was excruciating. But He was driven through His loss by the joy of what He was gaining. And what was that joy? Among other things, *you.*

This is the God who bids you to pick up your cross and follow Him.

Jesus is the treasure worth leaving everything for. Knowing Him will turn sacrifice into sweetness and duty into delight. Even when your commit-

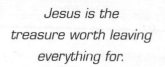

Jesus is the treasure worth leaving everything for.

ment to Him leads you to a cross, He will be a treasure that shrouds that cross in joy.

Loving Jesus is what makes Jesus' cross feel "light." How else could Jesus have said, "Come to me, all who labor and are heavy laden, and I will give you rest. . . . For my yoke is easy and my burden is light" (Matt. 11:28)? Isn't this the same Jesus who told us to take up our cross? How can the cross be a "light" burden?

Only when you love the One you are carrying it for. He makes even its bitterness sweet.

The point of this book is that the gospel is the only thing that can produce that kind of love for God in you. Love for Jesus cannot be produced simply by command. And without love, Paul said, even the greatest acts of faith and commitment are ultimately worthless to God (1 Cor. 13:1–3).

Love for God, Scripture says, flows from His love for us (1 John 4:19). The only way that love for God and others grows in us is through faith in the story of God's great love for us—the gospel.

As fallen people, we will certainly have to do a lot of things in our lives we don't feel like doing, even after we've gotten the gospel in the right place. We should do what's right whether we feel like it or not. But we should not be content simply to serve God with our actions while our heart wanders from Him. So as we discipline ourselves in doing what is right, let us also saturate our souls in the gospel so that we learn to love what is right. Our acts of obedience should in themselves be a cry of faith in the gospel.

Let the Law Be the Law, and the Gospel Be the Gospel[1]

Be very careful that you not use for prognosis what the Bible intends as diagnosis. Diagnosis describes what is wrong; prognosis tells us what to do about it.[2]

There are many things the Bible says will be true of us if our faith is genuine. I have explained many in this book: we will be generous with the poor (James 2:14–17); filled with love for the church (1 John 3:14); intensely concerned and working on behalf of the persecuted church (Matt. 25:31–46);

forgiving (Matt. 18:21–35); growing in our love for righteousness (1 John 3:3), and many other things. If these things are *not* true of us, then we may not be saved.

"Lovelessness," "apathy," and "habitual sin" are diagnoses of spiritual death. We go desperately wrong, however, when we think we can fix those things by correcting our behavior.

Faith in the gospel is always God's prognosis.

Jesus was once asked, "What must we do, to be doing the works of God?" (John 6:28). In other words, "What are the 'primary' works of God, Jesus, that you consider to be *most* important?" Is it *primarily* social justice, global missions, advocacy on behalf of the poor, Scripture memorization, church attendance, door-to-door visitation, small group participation—which is most important to You?

> *Faith in the gospel is always God's prognosis.*

Every church leader sits on the edge of their seat waiting to hear Jesus' answer. The answer determines the next big craze in Christianity.

Jesus identified none of these. He said, "This is the work of God, that you believe in him whom he has sent" (v. 29).

Wow. Our most important "doing" turns out to be "believing." When we have "done" that, of course, we will naturally start doing all the other stuff. Truly believing the gospel produces in us a concern for the poor, a love of Scripture, a desire to be in authentic community, a love for holiness, and everything else that is part of the Christian life. Those

> *Truly believing the gospel produces in us a concern for the poor, a love of Scripture, a desire to be in authentic community, a love for holiness, and everything else that is part of the Christian life.*

behaviors are the results of (or, fruits of) faith in the gospel. Believing precedes right behaving.

So, do you really want to do the works of God? Then believe on Him whom He has sent.

Believing the gospel is what released an explosive power in Jesus' followers that caused them to live with radical recklessness and audacious faith. It contradicted every other religious teaching in the world, in that it offered God's acceptance as a gift and not as a reward. That gift created an intensity and passion for God in Jesus' followers that no other religion was capable of producing.

Faith in the gospel released in Jesus' followers the power that made Christianity revolutionary.

So let me close by returning to the point I made at the beginning: Living a life centered on the gospel is not about praying the sinner's prayer to make sure you're going to heaven and then learning a bunch of new principles to master the Christian life. Gospel-centeredness is about saturating your heart in the good news of Jesus—letting it so remake your mind that you see everything about yourself and your life through its lens.

Growth in Christ is not going beyond the gospel, but deeper into it.

Make the gospel the center of your life. Turn to it when you are in pain. Let it be the foundation of your identity. Ground your confidence in it. Run to it when your soul feels restless. Take solace there in times of confusion and comfort there in times of regret. Dwell on it until righteous passions for God spring up within you. Let it inspire you to God-centered, death-defying dreams for His glory.

> *Believing the gospel is what released an explosive power in Jesus' followers that caused them to live with radical recklessness and audacious faith.*

My soul has found its resting place. No longer do I struggle, in anguish, over what I must do for God to be pleased with me. Christ has accomplished it all on my behalf. I can add nothing to it, and I can take nothing away. I have a lot of room to grow in my Christian life, but my position in Him is secure.

Having found (or better yet, been found by) Him, and overwhelmed at His grace, my heart is growing in love for Him and others. Generosity is like a stream that flows ever-stronger in my heart. I give away more money now than I ever have, not because I have to, but because I want to. I think about myself less now than I ever have—mainly because I have found a greater, more captivating kingdom to live for than my own. The splendor of His kingdom has made me bored with mine.

So, I invite you to dive deeper into the gospel. Study it, deeply—like the seminarian studies doctrine, but like you

study a sunset that leaves you speechless; or like a man who
is passionately in love with his wife studies her, until he's so
captivated by her that his enthrallment with her drives out any
allurements toward other women.[3]

The gospel is not merely the diving board off of which
you jumped into the pool of Christianity; the gospel is the
pool itself. So keep going deeper into it. You'll never find the
bottom.

I hope you'll pray this prayer with me for the rest of your
life!

"In Christ, there is nothing I can do
that would make You love me more, and nothing
I have done that makes You love me less."

"Your presence and approval are all
I need for everlasting joy."

"As You have been to me, so I will be to others."

"As I pray, I'll measure Your compassion by the cross
and Your power by the resurrection."

The Gospel Project

The gospel is the power of God for salvation. Nothing will alter your life more than dwelling on the richness of the gospel. It has happened to me; it's happened to our church; it will happen to you.

In light of that, I've got a challenge for you to complete as a follow-up to this book. Every day for the next forty days, will you (a) pray the four parts of The Gospel Prayer, and (b) read three chapters of the Gospels: Matthew, Mark, Luke, and John?

Why? I want you to saturate yourself in the gospel every day. The most gospel-centered books ever written are Matthew, Mark, Luke, and John. You'll find Jesus there. Dwell with Him in the Gospels for forty days, and let The Gospel Prayer saturate your heart and mind in His beauty and love. I think it will go a long way in helping you learn to "abide" in Him.

Again, here is the prayer:

> *"In Christ, there is nothing I can do*
> *that would make You love me more, and nothing*
> *I have done that makes You love me less."*

> *"Your presence and approval are all*
> *I need for everlasting joy."*

> *"As You have been to me, so I will be to others."*

> *"As I pray, I'll measure Your compassion by the cross*
> *and Your power by the resurrection."*

	Day	Reading
❑	1	Matthew 1–2
❑	2	Matthew 3–4
❑	3	Matthew 5–7
❑	4	Matthew 8–9
❑	5	Matthew 10–12
❑	6	Matthew 13–14
❑	7	Matthew 15–16
❑	8	Matthew 17–18
❑	9	Matthew 19–20
❑	10	Matthew 21–23
❑	11	Matthew 24–25
❑	12	Matthew 26–28
❑	13	Mark 1–3
❑	14	Mark 4–5
❑	15	Mark 6–7
❑	16	Mark 8–10
❑	17	Mark 11–13
❑	18	Mark 14–16
❑	19	Luke 1–2
❑	20	Luke 3–4

	Day	Reading
❑	21	Luke 5–6
❑	22	Luke 7
❑	23	Luke 8–9
❑	24	Luke 10–11
❑	25	Luke 12–13
❑	26	Luke 14–16
❑	27	Luke 17–19
❑	28	Luke 20–21
❑	29	Luke 22–24
❑	30	John 1–2
❑	31	John 3–4
❑	32	John 5–6
❑	33	John 7–8
❑	34	John 9–10
❑	35	John 11–12
❑	36	John 13–14
❑	37	John 15–16
❑	38	John 17
❑	39	John 18–19
❑	40	John 20–21

A Gospel-Centered Warning to Young Zealous Theologians

I've noticed that many of us who grasp this concept of "gospel-centeredness" can have a tendency to be more excited about the "theory" of gospel-centeredness than we are about the gospel itself. At least I'm that way. I have gotten pretty good at identifying non-gospel-centered preaching, and can pretty ably point out the shortcomings of certain ministries. The point of gospel-centeredness, however, is not the shrewd ability to critique others. The point of gospel-centeredness is to adore God and worship His grace.

> The point of gospel-centeredness is to adore God and worship His grace.

Many of us who love to talk about gospel-centeredness seem to possess very little of the humility that should go along with it. You can see that in how self-promoting we are and how ungracious we are with others. It always amazes me that we can be proud because we understand the very things that should lead us to humility.

My mind has often burned hotter with the latest theological trend than it has passion for the God who gave Himself for me at the cross. Knowledge that does not lead, ultimately, to love and humility is "worthless," Paul would say. What really counts, he says, is not knowledge by itself, but the love that our knowledge of the gospel should produce (1 Cor. 12:1–3).

One of my fears in writing this book is that it might contribute to a growing self-righteousness among younger theologians who feel like understanding gospel-centeredness makes them more special in the eyes of God (oh, the irony!) than those who can't articulate it, and who judge everyone else by whether or not they use the same terms that they do.

Recently I talked with a little old lady who had been my Sunday school teacher at the very traditional church in which I grew up. She said, "You know, as I lose more and more friends to heaven, I often wonder what it is really like up there and what I should be looking forward to. I know they say there are streets of gold, but that doesn't seem to excite me very much. The one thing I really want to do is see Jesus." This lady has never heard of John Piper and has no idea what the Gospel Coalition is, but she has been changed by the gospel. She loves Jesus, and that is the whole point of gospel-centeredness.

There are many little old ladies serving in church nurseries who may not understand how to articulate the theories of gospel-centeredness or have the ingenuity to dazzle our minds with psychological insights, cultural observations, and

Christocentric interpretations of obscure Old Testament passages. Their hearts, however, burn with love for Jesus and overflow with gratefulness for His grace.

Their humble, gospel-rich love for God is worth more than all the books you or I can write on this subject.

So don't be quick to judge them. Be humbled by them. Mastering the theory of gospel-centeredness is not the point. Loving the God of the gospel is.

Notes

Chapter 1

1. At this point, you may ask, "But why then are we commanded to love God, if true love only grows, naturally, as a response?" That is a great question, and one we will get to in time (specifically, chapter 12). The Bible certainly proscribes a lot of commandments, and we must obey them even when it means denying every passion we have to the contrary. As I'll explain in chapter 12, obeying God's commandments even when we don't feel like it can be in and of itself an act of faith in the gospel.

2. God gives the faith itself to believe in the gospel through the preaching of the gospel. The Spirit of God uses that message to impart the ability to believe to the hearers (John 1:13; John 6:44; Rom. 10:17). The specifics on when and how that happens believers may vary on, but most would agree that faith in the heart can only be produced through the power of the Spirit.

3. The first time I heard this particular phrasing was from a friend, Tullian Tchvidjian, in a message he gave at the Summit Church in 2010.

4. I owe this analogy to Paul Tripp, who gave it at a talk he gave at the Summit Church of Raleigh-Durham, North Carolina, in March, 2010.

5. The phrasing of this I owe to Tim Keller. As I said in the acknowledgments, it would be hard for me to overestimate the impact Dr. Keller, David Powlison, Ed Welch, and others have had on my thinking. They

have sent me through a gospel revolution I have never recovered from, and probably never will.

6. Martin Luther, *The Sermons of Martin Luther*, vol. VI (Grand Rapids: Baker, 1983), 146.

Chapter 2

1. I first heard these terms in Tim Keller's sermon on the parable of the seeds from Mark 4:3–20.

2. Paul says (Rom. 1:25) that the essence of human sin is worshipping and serving the creature more than the Creator. Adam and Eve ate of the forbidden fruit because they worshipped it in place of God.

3. The concepts "functional gods" and "functional saviors" are not original with me. Martin Luther, for example, talks about these concepts in his *Smaller Catechism*, and John Calvin does in the opening section of his *Institutes*. See also David Powlison, "Idols of the Heart and Vanity Fair," *The Journal of Biblical Counseling* 13:2 (Winter 1995), 35–50.

4. "Root idol" is a term coined by David Powlison in the article "Idols of the Heart and Vanity Fair," *Journal of Biblical Counseling*, vol. 13, no 2, Winter, 1995, 35.

5. Here again, I owe this concept to Tim Keller. Dr. Keller describes a similar situation in which he took classical music classes simply to get a grade, so he could get a job and make money. As he grew older, however, he developed a love for classical music that he now spends a lot of money to enjoy.

6. I first read this story in a sermon by Charles Spurgeon. I have also heard it told by D. Martyn-Lloyd Jones and Tim Keller. As I cannot find the original, some of the details I might have made up. The essence of the story, and the point Spurgeon was making with it, however, are the same. Keller's version is in *The Prodigal God: Recovering the Heart of the Christian Faith* (New York: Dutton, 2008), 60–62.

Chapter 3

1. Some scholars point out that the language here would be better translated, "*Since* You are the Son of God." As such, Satan may not be directly asking, "Are You sure You are the Son of God?" Rather, he is saying, "Since You are the Son of God . . . shouldn't You be able to make these circumstances different? You shouldn't be in the desert; You should

be sitting on a throne. You shouldn't be hungry; You should be feasting on bread." Either way, this is still an attack on Jesus' identity. Satan is subtly trying to get Jesus to question His identity by planting doubts about His circumstances. (Seen in this light, "If You are the Son of God," as many translations render it, would be more of a theological interpretation than a straight grammatical one. Jesus correctly rebuffs Satan's attack by feasting on God's declaration over Him as the validation of His identity, rather than on His present circumstances.)

2. This is from a sermon by Louie Giglio given at the Metro Bible Study in Atlanta, GA. Unfortunately, I cannot remember the sermon title.

3. See, for example, Martin Luther, *Luther's Works, Vol. 1: Lectures on Genesis: Chapters 1–5* (Saint Louis: Concordia Publishing House, 1999), 21–22. Carl Trueman, summarizing how Martin Luther thought about the power of words, "In other words, others might tell me I am a failure, an idiot, a clown, evil, incompetent, vicious, dangerous, pathetic, etc., and these words are not just descriptive: they have a certain power to make me these things, in the eyes of others and even in my own eyes, as self-doubt creeps in and the Devil whispers in my ear. But God speaks louder, and his word is more powerful. You may call me a liar, and you speak truth, for I have lied; but if God declares me righteous, then my lies and your insult are not the final word, nor the most powerful word. I have peace in my soul because God's word is real reality. That's why I need to read the Bible each day, to hear the word preached each week, to come to God in prayer, and to hear words of grace from other brothers and sisters as I seek to speak the same to them. Only as God speaks his word to me, and as I hear that word in faith, is my reality transformed and do the insults of others, of my own sinful nature, and of the evil one himself, cease to constitute my reality. The words of my enemies, external and internal, might be powerful for a moment, like a firework exploding against the night sky; but the Word of the Lord is stronger, brighter, and lasts forever." See http://www.reformation21.org/Upcoming_Issues/Buvvered/385.

Chapter 4

1. I am seeking to use "the law" as used by Paul in his letter to the Galatians. Under this usage, "obedience to the law" is that which seeks to change us by behavior modification rather than by faith in the gospel. The law tells us, Paul says, "do this and you shall live." Paul says this is the essence of works-righteousness. God changes us differently. Rather than

"do this and you shall live," the gospel says "the just shall live by faith" (Gal. 3:1–6, 11–13).

2. This is a point developed by a number of authors—Gary Thomas, John Eldredge, and Tim Keller, to name a few.

Chapter 5

1. I'm not sure who said this first, but I think the first time I heard this was by Mark Driscoll speaking at the Advance the Church conference in Durham, North Carolina.

2. For a complete study on idolatry, I would highly suggest Tim Keller's *Counterfeit Gods* (New York: Dutton, 2009).

3. For those of you who share that idol with me, I'd suggest *When People Are Big and God Is Small*, by Ed Welch (Phillipsburg: P&R Publishing, 1997). Welch offers a wonderfully insightful analysis of human nature, especially for driven, type-A people.

4. See C. S. Lewis, "The Weight of Glory," in *The Weight of Glory and Other Addresses* (New York: Simon & Schuster, 1975).

5. I've heard that imagery attributed to Jonathan Edwards, but am unsure of the source.

6. Inspiration for this came from a similar one given in a sermon by John Piper, "The Present Power of a Future Possession." See http://thegospelcoalition.org/blogs/justintaylor/2010/09/03/having-god-is-better-than-money-sex-power-or-popularity.

7. Lewis said this in a letter to Dom Bede Griffiths (April 23, 1951): "Put first things first and we get second things thrown in: put second things first and we lose *both* first and second things. We never get, say, even the sensual pleasure of food at its best when we are being greedy." He said something similar in "First and Second Things," in *God in the Dock: Essays on Theology and Ethics* (Grand Rapids: Eerdmans, 1994), 280.

Chapter 6

1. Explanation from Charles Misner, one of Einstein's students, on the reason why Einstein never believed in the Christian God. No source available.

2. Exodus 19:8; 24:3. Later, of course, they would renege on that pledge, falling about as far from God as possible. That was because the sight of God had faded from their eyes.

3. See www.firstthings.com/article/2007/12/the-feminist-revela tion-38.

Chapter 7

1. I have heard this interpretation of Jesus' words several times over the years, most recently from Tim Keller, Rob Bell, and Ken Sande. As with most of my interpretation in these pages, it is not original with me. Keller's sermons really help you understand grace-based forgiveness; Sande's book *Peacemaking for Families* (Wheaton: Tyndale, 2002) helps you apply the teaching in the context of relationships.

2. C. S. Lewis, *The Four Loves* (1960; Harcourt Brace: 1991), 105–6.

Chapter 8

1. Some readers may wonder if I am responding in this chapter to chapter 6 of David Platt's *Radical*, "How Much is Enough" (Colorado Springs: Multnomah Books, 2010), 111–44. The answer is "no," and "yes." "No," in that I have not attempted in this chapter fully or fairly to recount David's ideas about money and respond to them. "Yes," in that some readers of Platt's book have adopted an imbalanced view of money and God's purposes for it in our lives. I have written this chapter to clarify what I believe the Bible teaches about money. Platt reviewed this chapter and told me that he is in agreement with the basic principles presented. David and I both believe that godly friendship and godly critique are not at odds, and I am grateful for *Radical* and the impact it has had on world missions. I believe, with David, that the soul of the American church has been captivated by "the American dream," and pray that God give our generation the grace to love what Jesus loves and leverage our resources in pursuit of those things.

2. John Calvin, *Institutes of the Christian Religion*, ed. John T. McNeill (1559, reprinted Philadelphia: Westminster, 1960), 1:839.

3. You won't find a better study on the Christian's obligation to the poor, in my opinion, than Tim Keller's *Generous Justice: How God's Grace Makes Us Just* (New York: Dutton, 2010). Run, don't walk, to the bookstore to get your copy.

4. John 14:18, 28. I know I am treading on dangerous ground here. *How* exactly the Spirit guides is a complex, biblically rich discussion. If this is a real point of question for you, again, let me suggest Kevin DeYoung's

Just Do Something: a Liberating Approach to Finding God's Will (Chicago: Moody, 2009). There are few resources on this subject as well-balanced and easy-to-read as Kevin's.

5. For a good additional resource on this topic, read Randy Alcorn's *Money, Possessions and Eternity* (Wheaton: Tyndale, 2002), 285. The whole book is excellent, but I found particularly helpful chapter 16, "Making Money, Owning Possessions, and Choosing a Lifestyle," from which this observation comes.

6. For more on this principle, see Gary Thomas' *Pure Pleasure: Why Do Christians Feel So Bad About Feeling Good?* (Grand Rapids: Zondervan, 2009), chapters 3, 5, and 11. Personally, I find Thomas to be a little out of balance, and not giving enough weight to the Christian's call to suffer and sacrifice. Thomas lays out the biblical case for enjoyment of God's good gifts, though.

7. This came from a personal conversation I had with Larry Osborne, senior pastor of North Coast Church in Vista, California, in May 2010.

8. I owe the connection of flowers to beauty and ravens to security to a message by Tim Keller on the passage given at Redeemer Presbyterian in New York City.

9. This is from Randy Alcorn's *Treasure Principle* (Colorado Springs: Multnomah, 2005), 17, another of Alcorn's works on money which I would heartily recommend to you.

Chapter 9

1. If you find the idea that people can only be saved by calling on the name of Jesus troubling, you might read John Piper's *Jesus: The Only Way to God. Must You Hear the gospel to Be Saved?* (Grand Rapids: Baker, 2010), or chapter 7 in David Platt's *Radical: Taking Back Your Faith from the American Dream* (Colorado Springs: Multnomah, 2010). I've taught myself on that in a message entitled "The Task Is Urgent: Romans 10:14–17," given at the Summit Church in Durham, North Carolina, on October 3, 2010. It is available for free download at www.summitrdu.com.

2. See the discussion in chapter 10. See also Acts 13:1–3. The early church was eager to see the gospel sent forward to the nations, but they waited on the Holy Spirit to direct them and empower them to do the work. This is just what Jesus had taught them to do (Acts 1:6–8).

3. He used a technical Islamic term for "the straight path" which applies only to the road to heaven.

Chapter 10

1. That's what Jesus told His disciples in John 6. The greatest "work of God" that we are supposed to do is believe Him. Believing is what empowers all other works, because believing releases what God will do in the situation (John 6:29).

2. The Bible teaches two complementary, not contradictory, truths. On one hand, God is completely sovereign over all who will be saved, and not one is lost (John 6:37, 44), and even if we do not play our role in preaching salvation to them, God will raise up someone else to do it in our place (Esther 4:14–16). The complementary truth is that if we do not go, those who might have been saved won't be saved because they won't have a chance to hear (Rom. 10:14–17), and we will be guilty of their blood (Ezek. 33:1–0; Acts 20:26–27). For us to be "blood guilty" means that had we done our duty, their life might have been saved. We must believe and hold both in tension.

3. Hudson Taylor's *Spiritual Secret*, chapters 11 and 19, http://www.woobiola.net/books/taylor/jhtsecr.htm.

4. From William Carey, Father of the Protestant Missions movement.

Chapter 11

1. Two great books that will take you more into God's purposes in suffering and evil are Randy Alcorn's *If God Is Good: Faith in the Midst of Suffering and Evil* (Colorado Springs: Multnomah, 2009) and D. A. Carson's *How Long, O Lord? Reflections on Suffering and Evil* (Grand Rapids: Baker, 1990).

Chapter 12

1. Again, I owe this analogy to Tullian Tchvidjian.

2. This quote comes from Jerry Bridges' excellent book, *The Discipline of Grace* (Colorado Springs: NavPress, 1994). I owe a great debt to Bridges for this book, as well as his *Transforming Grace* (Colorado Springs: NavPress, 2008).

3. Chip and Dan Heath make this point in a secular context in their recently released leadership book, *Switch: How to Change Things When Change Is Hard* (Crown Business, 2010). They explain how effective leaders implement change in organizations. They make the case that we can

promote change more by changing what people experience than by convincing them of the need for change. They compare it to a man riding an elephant who is guiding the elephant with reins. The rider might think he's directing the animal, but if the animal itself ever decided to go a new direction, the rider would be helpless to actually stop it. In their analogy, the elephant is like our desires, the rider is like our mind. There are two ways to make the rider go a certain direction. You can tell him to go that direction, and hope he can persuade the animal. Or, you can persuade the animal, and the rider will have to follow.

4. Paul Miller's *A Praying Life* (Colorado Springs: NavPress, 2009) is an excellent resource on a number of levels. His treatment of prayer and spiritual disciplines is among the best I've ever read.

5. An excellent treatment of fasting and the whole concept of spiritual discipline is John Piper's *Hunger for God* (Wheaton, IL: Crossway, 1997).

6. A friend of mine applies this principle (that you can teach the heart to love something by active participation in it) in a fascinating way to evangelism. Pastor Bob Roberts says that the most effective way to change a skeptic's mind is usually not through argument, but through his hands. If you have an atheist, Bob says, who is not open to God at all, invite them to serve the poor with you. As they experience the joy of giving to someone else, their heart becomes softened to God, because God is love. As they experience sacrificial love, they are experiencing a dimension of God. That makes their hearts more receptive to God, which makes their minds more receptive to arguments for God. Hands—heart—heads. What they love, and even what they think, comes from what they were experiencing and doing. Bob Roberts is one of the most effective evangelists that I know.

Chapter 13

1. To get a good handle on how God directs us today, start by doing a study on how to discern the will of God in your life. (I would suggest Kevin DeYoung's *Just Do Something* (Chicago: Moody, 2009) coupled with Henry Blackaby's classic *Experiencing God* (Nashville: B&H Publishing Group, 1998). Both books have limitations, in my opinion, but together I believe that they will raise some good questions and point you in the right direction.)

2. Tim Keller's *Generous Justice* (New York: Dutton Adult, 2010) can help you consider what this looks like for you and your church.

3. I'd suggest you do a study on how God uses secular vocations in His kingdom, such as Gene Edward Veith's *God at Work* (Wheaton, IL: Crossway, 2002).

4. See http://www.modernreformation.org/default.php?page=articled isplay&var1=ArtRead&var2=1201&var3=main.

Chapter 14

1. Michael Horton, *Christless Christianity* (Grand Rapids: Baker, 2008), 119.

2. The traditional "5 points of Calvinism" are "Total Depravity"; "Unconditional Election"; "Limited Atonement"; "Irresistible Grace"; and "Perseverance of the Saints."

3. 1 John 3:16–18. God's sacrifice for the world flowed out of His love for it. Our sacrifices for the world should demonstrate our love as well. John is saying that love without sacrifice is worthless (1 John 3:16–18), but Paul tells us that so is sacrifice without love (1 Cor. 13:1–3).

4. Arthur W. Pink, *An Exposition of Hebrews* (Grand Rapids: Baker, 2003), 601.

5. Horton, *Christless Christianity*, 143–44.

6. Rodney Stark, "Urban Chaos and Crises: The Case of Antioch," in *The Rise of Christianity* (San Francisco: HarperCollins, 1997), 156–72.

7. This is not, of course, to deny, that there were some truly unique things happening in the earliest days of Christianity. I do believe God did some special things to authenticate the message of the apostles, as passages like Hebrews 2:1–4 seem to indicate. That does not, however, mean we cannot ask for, and expect, God to do miraculous things in our midst too.

8. *Preaching and Preachers* (Grand Rapids: Zondervan, 1971), 23.

9. "Church Efforts Earn Family Status at Elementary School," *Biblical Recorder*, vol. 175, no. 19 (12 September 2009), 7.

Conclusion

1. I owe this phrasing to Michael Horton, *Christless Christianity*, (Grand Rapids: Baker, 2008), 124.

2. This mistake made the uber-zealous Pharisees the "two-fold children of hell" and haters of Jesus Christ (Matt. 23:15).

3. I owe this analogy for passionate study to the masterful work of Peter Kreeft in his clever little book *Between Allah and Jesus* (Downers Grove: IVP, 2010).

Start a revolution.

Introduce your church to the power of the Gospel Prayer.

If after reading this book, you're already seeing positive changes in yourself, imagine what would happen if everyone in your church experienced these teachings. So why not multiply the message of *Gospel Revolution* through an 8-session Bible study? The *Member Book* expands on the principles featured in the book, offering personal devotionals, leader notes, and discussion questions that take groups into a deeper dive of the revolutionary message of the gospel. The DVD includes eight video teaching sessions that complement the group experience with unique insights from the author. It also contains sermon outlines and many promotional tools to get your entire church excited about doing the study. Visit us online to see free sample chapters and video.

HCSB
_____
Take a
fresh look

Every word matters.

Every word of Scripture matters because every word is from God and for people. Because every word is from God, the HCSB uses words like Yahweh (Is. 42:8), Messiah (Luke 3:15), and slave (Rev. 1:1). And because every word of Scripture is for 21st century people, the HCSB replaces words like "Behold" with modern terms like "Look." For these reasons and others, Christians across the globe are taking a fresh look at the HCSB.

HCSB
Every Word Matters
HCSB.org